Decision Making

Stephen P. Fitzgerald

- ■ Fast track route to mastering business decision making

- ■ Covers the key areas of decision making, from decision support systems and global templates to contemplation and implementation

- ■ Examples and lessons from some of the world's most successful businesses, including Coca Cola and Pepsi Cola, The Valio Group, Best Buy, and Scandic Hotels, and ideas from the smartest thinkers, including Mary Altomare, Mike Aristedes, David L. Cooperrider, Andre L. Delbecq, J. D. Eveland, Brian Hsieh, Don Mankin, Paul Nutt, Daniel Power, and Morris Raker

- ■ Includes a glossary of key concepts and a comprehensive resources guide.

LEADING

08.07

>> EXPRESS EXEC.COM <<
essential management thinking at your fingertips

T0341715

First published 2002 by
Capstone Publishing (a Wiley company)
8 Newtec Place
Magdalen Road
Oxford OX4 1RE
United Kingdom
http://www.capstoneideas.com

CIP catalogue records for this book are available from the British Library and the US Library of Congress

ISBN 1-84112-255-6

This book is printed on acid-free paper

Contents

To my dad, now lost to Alzheimer's, for being such an all around great decision-maker.

Introduction to ExpressExec

ExpressExec is 3 million words of the latest management thinking compiled into 10 modules. Each module contains 10 individual titles forming a comprehensive resource of current business practice written by leading practitioners in their field. From brand management to balanced scorecard, ExpressExec enables you to grasp the key concepts behind each subject and implement the theory immediately. Each of the 100 titles is available in print and electronic formats.

Through the ExpressExec.com Website you will discover that you can access the complete resource in a number of ways:

» printed books or e-books;
» e-content – PDF or XML (for licensed syndication) adding value to an intranet or Internet site;
» a corporate e-learning/knowledge management solution providing a cost-effective platform for developing skills and sharing knowledge within an organization;
» bespoke delivery – tailored solutions to solve your need.

Why not visit www.expressexec.com and register for free key management briefings, a monthly newsletter and interactive skills checklists. Share your ideas about ExpressExec and your thoughts about business today.

Please contact elound@wiley-capstone.co.uk for more information.

Introduction

Given the decades of research on decision making and its vital importance to business, why do so many key managerial decisions fail? Recent research is presented that sheds light on answers to that question. The central role of decision making in management and the forces that are shaping it in the new millennium are also discussed.

If you're a business manager, executive, or leader at any level, you're doing it. You're doing it all day, every day – and all-too-frequently all night in this increasingly non-stop global marketplace. It's what you get paid the big bucks for (or not). In fact, it's widely considered to be *the primary function* that distinguishes management from non-management (at least within more traditional organizational settings in which that distinction still exists). "It" is making business decisions.

Making business decisions is the bread and butter of everyday organizational management. It ranks alongside leadership as one of the core topics of vital, perennial interest to business. In fact, it is so crucial to human endeavor that an entire scientific discipline is devoted to studying and improving decision-making processes. Legions of management thinkers, tinkerers, and sorcerers draw upon the fruits of that and other relevant research (to a greater or lesser extent), combine it with healthy doses of practical wisdom, skepticism, and sleight-of-hand, and presto! They transform it all into a wild and ever-escalating cacophony of decision-making theories, models, processes, tools, techniques, and approaches.

For example, a quick search for "decision making" on Amazon.com yields a whopping 6681 books – with 1126 of those categorized under business and investing, 1362 under professional and technical, and 761 under non-fiction, and those numbers continue to escalate. The books cover all sectors (private, public, and non-profit). They range from classic texts that mine ancient wisdom about purportedly related topics like Sun Tzu's *The Art of War*[1] (no less than 49 different versions and derivatives of this book are available), to primers on various facets of decision making and analysis,[2] to current treatises on critical issues like business and the environment.[3] Add to that at least 734 articles on business decision making that have been published since 1986 (with 170 of those appearing since 1999) according to a search on Proquest, and 12,300 Web page matches on a Yahoo.com search that only begins to touch upon the number of consultants, courses, and other resources on business decision making that are available.

This cornucopia of decision-making guidance and "support" can obviously overwhelm the unsuspecting manager. It can lead to decisional gridlock. What's needed is a book, tool, or technique to help us wade through these mountains of models, tools, techniques, and approaches, and to help us decide which to rely on – if any. Unfortunately such an analysis is impractical if not impossible, and certainly beyond the scope of this brief volume.

The bounty of resources on decision making reflects its central importance to the field of management. Curiously, while management is eternal and all-embracing, debates continue to rage (typically among academics, not among managers) as to what does and should actually constitute management. The host of definitions now available cannot cloud the central fact that management is about decision making. "Decisions are the essence of management," says Des Dearlove, author of *The Ultimate Book of Business Thinking: Harnessing the Power of the World's Greatest Business Ideas*.[4] "Management without decision making is a vacuum. Of course, that does not mean that every decision a manager makes is important or that they always make the right decisions. The vast majority of decisions made by managers are completely unimportant. And often the decisions they make are the wrong ones."[5]

Wrong or right, an astonishing 50% of senior management decisions fail, according to a 1999 study of 356 highly diverse, actual decisions made in medium to large private, public, and non-profit organizations throughout the US and Canada.[6] The researcher, Ohio State Professor Paul Nutt, has been studying managerial decision making for twenty years. He finds that "managers often jump to conclusions and then try to implement the solution they reached. The bias for action causes them to limit their search, consider too few alternatives, and pay too little attention to people who are affected, not realizing that decisions fail for just these reasons." Nutt identifies several underlying reasons for decision failure.

1 As time pressures intensify (a key mantra in business today, and a by-product of globalization and technological innovation), managers take "time-saving" shortcuts, like quickly attempting to copy the best practice of a respected company. Unfortunately, such "time-savers" often lead to unexpected, costly complications – including decision failure.

2 Instead of communicating the criteria for desired solutions to their subordinates and liberating them to generate creative alternatives, managers tend to rely on problem-solving approaches, not realizing

that those approaches only generate defensiveness and blaming behavior among subordinates.

3 Managers fail to use the most successful approaches to setting the direction for a decision-making process because they "are drawn to power and shy away from ambiguity and uncertainty."

4 Although managers are commonly aware of some higher quality approaches to decision making like participation, they tend to resort to more ineffective approaches like issuing edicts. For example, participation was used in just 1 out of 5 of the 356 significant decisions included in the study. Yet 73% of decisions made with participation were fully implemented, and 80% of those decisions continued to be sustained after two years, as opposed to a mere 35% and 53% for decisions made by edict, and 47% and 56% for decisions made via persuasion. Unfortunately, the latter two methods were employed 75% of the time.

Think about those numbers for a minute. Edict and persuasion – the approaches to implementing decisions favored by 3 out of 4 senior managers in a highly diverse sample of organizations and types of decisions – failed in 65% and 53% of those decisions, respectively. These failure rates are even more shocking when considered in light of the plethora of resources on effective decision making described above.

Ultimately, the costs associated with such high failure rates are staggering. Surely with all of the decision-making research, models, tools, and techniques available, we should be able to do *better* – not worse – than a simple coin flip, shouldn't we? As Paul Nutt notes, *there are demonstrably better ways to make decisions*. However, we must have the courage to step out of our comfort zones and try something different – and significantly more effective. Managers have some important decisions to make about how they make decisions.

Those choices will become increasingly critical as the constellation of factors affecting business decisions continues to broaden, deepen, and intensify. Those factors include the usual suspects:

» continually accelerating pace of change;
» relentless technological innovation, including e-commerce;
» rapid transformation to an information-based, knowledge economy;

» escalating demand for and shortage of knowledge workers;
» demands to globalize, localize, diversify, and right-size – often simultaneously; and
» constantly shifting markets, organizational structures and boundaries.

If edicts didn't work very well in the old economy, think about trying to implement a decision by decree in a virtual network organization. Think about trying to make the decision alone – quickly and effectively – based on the information you have in your head. Business decisions in the twenty-first century demand instant access to extensive, relevant, high-quality data – anywhere, anytime. They increasingly require respectful collaboration with diverse others, a facilitative leadership style, and equanimity in the midst of turmoil. And as the need for collaboration escalates, it's important to be able to understand and work effectively with others' decision styles, as well as to choose and shape yours appropriately.

This book is designed to stimulate thinking regarding the intricacies of effective decision making. We'll begin with a very brief overview of some of the basic ideas and theories associated with business decision making, and a quick look at its evolution. We'll then explore the implications of e-commerce, globalization, and leading-edge thinking and practice in making business decisions. Three success stories from highly complex business environments are then discussed, followed by a glossary, and links to a wide variety of Web-based resources. We'll conclude by considering ten steps to help heighten the effectiveness of your business decision making. Each chapter can stand alone, and chapters may be taken out of sequence and at random, to suit your particular interests and needs.

If ever in doubt, you might just try flipping a coin, as you are likely to beat the prevailing track record of senior decision-makers. Otherwise, read on – but save that coin as a backup.

NOTES

1 See, for example, Sun Tzu (1988) *The Art of Strategy: A New Translation of Sun Tzu's Classic, the Art of War*, Wing, R.L. (trans). Doubleday, New York.

2 See, for example, Sinner, D. (1999) *Introduction to Decision Analysis*, 2nd edn. Probabilistic Publishing, New York

3 See, for example, Gordon, P. (2001) *Lean and Green: Profit for Your Workplace and the Environment*. Berrett-Koehler, San Francisco, CA.

4 Dearlove, D. (2001) *The Ultimate Book of Business Thinking: Harnessing the Power of the World's Greatest Business Ideas*. Capstone Publishing, Oxford.

5 Author interview.

6 Nutt, P. (1999) "Surprising but true: Half the decisions in organizations fail." *Academy of Management Executive*, **13**(4).

Definition of Terms: What is Decision Making?

All managerial decisions are not alike. They differ significantly in their nature, scope, and potential impact. Decision making and related terms are defined, and several of the key conceptual models of decision making are briefly discussed.

- » Defining decision making
- » Nature, scope, and types of managerial decisions
- » Decision scope and allocation of resources
- » Models of decision making
- » Key learning points

"The essence of ultimate decision-making remains impenetrable to the observer – often indeed, to the decider himself ... There will always be the dark and tangled stretches in the decision-making process – mysterious even to those who may be most intimately involved."

John F. Kennedy[1]

All decisions are not alike. Distinguishing the nature of a decision – prior to launching into one's favored decision-making approach or deciding whether to try a new one – may facilitate the process of deciding and implementing. It can aid in identifying stakeholders that should optimally have input into the process and/or be informed of its progress and outcomes. It can help define the scope of the decision, and the context which gives rise to the decision opportunity.

In this chapter we will:

» define managerial decision making;
» gain an understanding of the nature and types of decisions that managers make;
» explore the concept of decision scope and its implications for the level of resources (information, people, time, money, technology) that may be called for in decision situations;
» compare several basic models of decision making; and
» contrast individual and group decision making.

The intent is to provide the reader with an overview of basic ideas related to managerial decision making as a resource for enhancing the quality and effectiveness of his or her business decisions.

DEFINING DECISION MAKING

Making a decision involves a choice among alternatives. A managerial decision typically commits organizational resources to a course of action in order to accomplish something that the organization (and/or the manager) desires and values.

A decision is the point at which a choice is made between alternative – and usually competing – options. As such, it may be seen as a stepping-off point – the moment at which a commitment is made to one course of action to the exclusion of others. In practice, it is the commitment made to a particular course of action that imbues a decision with significance.

It is no coincidence that the word decision actually means "to cut," or as Helga Drummond says in her book *Effective Decision-Making*,[2] "to resolve upon a specific choice or course of action." Drummond makes an important distinction between a decision *per se*, and the decision-making process. The decision, she suggests, is the final outcome of the process, but the decision-making process involves "events leading up to the moment of choice and beyond." This is a valid point. However, as with so many processes which take place in the human brain, it is difficult – if not impossible – to entirely separate cause from effect. In addition, simply making a decision does not guarantee its successful implementation, as any experienced manager can attest.

Thus making business decisions involves processes that precede the actual decision, including gathering information and generating, contemplating, and evaluating alternative courses of action, as well as processes of implementation and evaluation that should follow a decision once made. Improving the quality of business decisions, therefore, involves a spectrum of processes that must be taken into account.

NATURE, SCOPE, AND TYPES OF MANAGERIAL DECISIONS

Virtually all decisions we make are managerial in nature. Decisions usually concern people (human resources); money (budgeting); buying and selling (marketing); how to do things (operations); or how to do things in the future (strategy and planning). These may be more broadly classified into two generic types of decisions.

» *Routine*: Decisions that need to be made on a recurring basis. Organizations may develop and implement systems to support managers in handling such repetitive decision situations.
» *Non-routine*: Unique, random, non-recurring decision situations. Such non-routine decisions typically have strategic implications for the organization.

The routine/non-routine categorization is similar – but not identical – to another common way of classifying business decisions as being either operational or strategic in nature.

» *Operational decisions* are concerned with the day-to-day running of the business. While operational decisions have a greater tendency to fall into the routine category, not all do. Examples of operational decisions might include setting production levels, deciding to recruit additional employees, or deciding whether to close a particular factory.
» *Strategic decisions* are those concerned with organizational policy and direction over a longer time period. So a strategic decision might involve determining whether to enter a new market, acquire a competitor, or exit from an industry altogether.

Interestingly, Madan G. Singh, chair of information engineering at Manchester University's Institute of Science and Technology and an acknowledged expert on decision making, prefers an alternative breakdown of decision levels, which recognizes some of the changes taking place within companies.[3] He divides the decision-makers in an organization into three levels of decisions.

» *Day-to-day decisions* are those made by front-line staff. Collectively, they make thousands of decisions daily, most of them in a short timeframe and on the basis of concrete information – answering a customer's request for information about a product, for example. Their decisions usually have a narrow scope and influence a small range of activities.
» *Tactical decisions* cover a few weeks to a few months, and include decisions such as the pricing of goods and services, and deciding advertising and marketing expenditures.
» *Strategic decisions* are those with the longest time horizon – one to five years or longer. They generally concern expanding or contracting the business, or entering new geographic or product markets.

Tactical and strategic decisions not only have longer-term implications, the data needed to make them are much broader, extending outside the organization, and the information derived from that data is less precise, less current, and subject to more error. This classification is based upon the relative scope of decisions.

Decision scope

Decision scope may be thought of as the extent of the potential impact of a decision. For example, the consequences of a particular decision may affect one person or millions, one pound/dollar or millions, one product/service or an entire market, one day or 10 years, and so on, depending upon the nature of that decision. Decisions with the broadest scope are typically made by those in the top echelons of an organization, although forward thinking organizations are increasingly involving all levels of personnel in broad-scope decision processes in order to ensure that important data is not overlooked, and to facilitate implementation of the decision once it has been made.

Exactly what constitutes a broad-scope decision will depend upon the size and nature of the business. For example, for a small firm an investment of £10,000 might be a big decision, while for a multinational it would barely be a drop in the ocean. (On the other hand, the same investment may represent a big decision for a very junior manager even though its impact on the organization is limited to his or her immediate career prospects.) Thus decision scope is relative, not absolute. It depends entirely upon the context within which the decision is being made, and the characteristics of the person(s) making the decision. The general principle holds, however, that some decisions are of a greater magnitude or scope than others.

Decision scope and allocation of resources

Understanding the scope of a decision can aid in determining the resources (e.g. people, information, time, money, technology) that should be allocated to it. For example, it makes no sense to devote a lot of resources to a decision with a very narrow scope – *unless* it happens to be the sort of routine, narrow-scope decision that is made by hundreds or thousands of personnel on a frequent basis. In that case, investment in technical support systems and training to provide ready access to information that those decision-makers need to have on hand is essential. But a decision that potentially impacts hundreds or thousands of narrow-scope decisions is in fact a non-routine decision of relatively broad scope. Thus it is essential to clarify the nature and scope of the decision situation in order to develop appropriate solutions and resource commitments.

MODELS OF DECISION MAKING

Models are conceptualizations intended to represent complex phenomena, and to assist us in understanding those phenomena. By their very nature models are gross simplifications. They may be descriptive (this is how decisions are made in the real world), predictive/prescriptive (following this model will increase the likelihood of making a "successful" decision), and/or normative (there is one best way to make decisions). Models typically exclude as much as they include, therefore every model should be viewed with a healthy dose of skepticism.

Once a model becomes popular, it influences the way that we perceive things, and in some ways models may actually shape our experience of organizational "reality." Thus they are not mere representations. They can have a significant impact on the way managers think and act. Beware the seemingly innocuous model!

Rational model

The most pervasive and influential (for better or worse) model of decision making is the rational approach that consists of a logical sequence of five steps (depending on who's counting).

1 Clearly identify the problem. A "problem" may be defined as a perceived gap between the current and desired reality, hence "gap analysis" as a standard approach to problem identification.
2 Generate potential solutions. For routine decisions, various alternatives may be fairly easily identified through pre-specified decision rules, but non-routine decisions require a creative process to come up with novel alternatives.
3 Using appropriate analytic approaches, choose a solution from among the available alternatives, preferably the one with the greatest expected value. In decision theory this is called maximizing the "expected utility" of the results.

4 Implement the solution. Managers frequently undermine implementation by not ensuring that those responsible for the implementation fully understand and accept what they need to do, and that they have the motivation and resources needed to do it successfully.[4]

5 Evaluate the effectiveness of the implemented decision.

Embedded within the rational model is the belief that managers actually *optimize* their decision-making behaviors by deliberately choosing and implementing the best alternatives.[5] But the belief in the ability to optimize is based on a host of dubious assumptions, including that:

» it is possible to know in advance all of the possible alternative solutions and the specific results that will flow from each of them;

» there is in fact an optimal solution, and that solution is included among the alternatives that have been identified;

» it is possible to accurately, numerically weight the various alternatives, the probabilities of their outcomes, and the relative desirability of those alternatives and outcomes;

» decision-makers always act rationally, and therefore decision making is free of emotion, prejudice, and politics; and

» business decisions are entirely driven by the desire to maximize profits.

The rational model is normative in that it sets forth a logical sequence of steps to be followed religiously in every decision situation. It is built on the foundations set down by economists in the early industrial period. They believed that under a given set of circumstances human behavior is logical and therefore predictable. Based on this premise, they built models to explain the workings of commerce, which they believed could be extended to the way in which decisions were made.

Simon's normative model

Nearly a quarter century ago, in 1978, decision theorist Herbert Simon won the Nobel Prize for his groundbreaking theoretical work on decision making. In Simon's view "the assumptions of perfect rationality are contrary to fact. It is not a question of approximation; they do not even remotely describe the processes that human beings use for making decisions in complex situations.''[6] Simon proposed that decision making is constrained by managers' limited ability to process information (which he called ''bounded rationality'') and their use of shortcuts and rules of thumb based on prior experience with problems that seem similar to the current situation. Given these constraints, in real life managers don't actually optimize as much as they '' *satisfice*,'' that is, they choose a solution that is just good enough to solve the problem and get on with it. It's a satisfactory solution, not necessarily the best or optimal solution (if there even is such a thing). This is a descriptive model in that it attempts to illustrate how managers actually make decisions in the ''real world.''

Garbage Can model

This is the name given to a pattern of decision making in organizations first identified by the American Professor of Management James March.[7] It is a descriptive model in which organizational ''participants'' generate a constant stream of problems and solutions when faced with a decision or ''choice opportunity.'' These streams – participants, problems, solutions, and choice opportunities – are metaphorically ''dumped'' into an organizational ''garbage can,'' the four streams interact at random, and only a very small percentage of the solutions generated are ever incorporated in the final decision.

The Garbage Can model also implies that participants seize upon problems as opportunities to implement their favorite solutions, which in turn are based on their experience and personal style. Thus another way to view this model is to see organizations as sets of competing solutions – each favored by different participants – waiting for problems to arise. Decisions may then be regarded as what happens when a set of problems, solutions, and choices come together – or collide – at a particular juncture. In a sense, the final decision is no more than the by-product of the alchemy that take place within the organizational ''garbage can.''

Thinking, seeing, and doing

In spite of Herbert Simon's decades-old Nobel Prize-winning observations on the limitations of rational decision making, the rational model is tenacious. It continues to pervade management approaches to decision making in spite of its obvious and well-documented limitations, as well as the introduction of sundry alternative models. Perhaps, however, the answer lies not in abandoning the rational model as being hopelessly flawed, but rather in supplementing it with missing elements that will help it to more closely approximate actual decision processes and provide for greater flexibility. For example, Henry Mintzberg and Frances Westley[8] suggest augmenting the rationalistic "thinking first" approach with two others: "seeing first" and "doing first."

Seeing first involves insight accessed through visioning and imagination. It is the realm of art and ideas. Doing first involves learning through doing, actively exploring alternatives, and experimenting with them to discover what works. It is the realm of experience, more akin to the world of craft than to that of art or science. In contrast, thinking first is rooted in facts and logical planning processes. It is more science than art or craft.

Each approach has pros and cons that tend to complement the other two. Mintzberg and Westley advocate the application of thinking to well-structured decision situations in which problems are clearly identified, adequate and reliable data are available, and discipline may be employed. An example might be a decision regarding an existing production process.

In contrast, a seeing first approach should be utilized for situations like developing new products that require a lot of boundary-spanning communication in order to integrate a variety of elements into creative solutions, and a strong need for commitment to those solutions. Mintzberg and Westley have managers develop their capacity for a seeing first approach by asking them to create a collage together as a group. The collage represents an issue that they have previously addressed through a verbally based, thinking first approach.

Managers report that having to create a picture together requires reaching consensus. It reveals underlying issues that tend to be overlooked in entirely rational approaches.

The emotions and imagination are engaged in addition to the intellect, and the image created leaves a far more lasting impression than flip charts with logically sequenced bullet points ever could.

Managers should do first, before analyzing or visualizing, when the decision situation is puzzling and unique, and when the way forward is not clear. In these situations it will be more helpful to implement a few simple relationship guidelines than a set of complex, detailed plans and specifications. Typical applications occur in new industries, or in an established industry thrown into turmoil by new technology.

Companies can no longer rely on any single decision-making approach, according to Mintzberg and Westley, and should ideally incorporate all three. They should use art/seeing to envision the way forward, science/thinking to structure their plans to get there, and craft/doing to actually make it to the collectively envisioned destination.

Individual vs. group decision making: the Decision-Making Model

Ironically, managers need to make a host of decisions in the processes that precede the focal decision or "choice opportunity." For example, managers must determine the range, quality, and specificity of information that may be required. They must also choose among available sources for that information. They may draw upon internal and external data sources, and their own experience and intuition as well as that of others. Perhaps most importantly, managers must determine when to involve others in decision-making processes, and to what extent.

The Decision-Making Model (Victor Vroom and Philip Yetton,[9] Vroom and Arthur Jago[10]) can guide managers in choosing the level of involvement of others in decision making to appropriately match the characteristics of a particular decision situation. The model is normative, predictive, and prescriptive, and its effectiveness has been supported by several research studies.[11] Vroom and Yetton differentiated five possible levels of involvement in decision making, ranging from completely autocratic to completely participatory. They viewed these as styles or strategies that managers could choose to utilize according to the demands of the decision situation.

The first two styles are autocratic in that the leader/manager makes the decision alone, but in the second autocratic approach the leader solicits information from his or her staff. The third and fourth styles are consultative, the leader also makes the decision alone, but consults his or her staff to an increasing degree in preparation for making the decision. It is only in the fifth style that the decision is actually made by the consensus of the group.

The model employs a "decision tree" (refer to the glossary in Chapter 8) to guide managers through a series of specific yes/no, high/low questions which ultimately lead to the selection of a decision-making style that is deemed appropriate for the particular situation. The questions include the following.[9]

» Does the situation require a "high quality" decision?
» Do you have enough information to make a high quality decision (if needed)?
» Is the problem structured?
» Is acceptance of the decision by your subordinates essential for its effective implementation?
» Will your subordinates accept the decision if you make it by yourself?
» Are organizational goals shared by your subordinates?
» Is the favored solution likely to cause conflict among your subordinates?

Even thinking through these questions informally can help clarify how much to involve others in the decision-making process. A significant drawback to the model is its complexity, which can make it difficult for managers to comprehend and use. Unfortunately, more recent elaborations of the model by Vroom and Jago have made it even more complex, although perhaps more accurate as well.

Overall, the reality is that decision making is an art not a science. Effective decision-makers realize this and balance a number of elements. These include the need not only for hard data and rigorous analysis, but also for softer, less tangible aspects such as intuition, experience, and moral and ethical judgments.

To view decision making as a hard discipline is to miss the subtleties of the art. One way to think about this is to consider logic, intuition, and experience as three sides of a "decision triangle." Effective decision making involves balancing three elements: logic, intuition, and experience. Each of these has a bearing on the way we understand the issues involved and reach our conclusions.

KEY LEARNING POINTS
Decision: a choice among alternatives
Classifications of business decisions include:

» Routine – non-routine
» Operational – strategic
» Day-to-day, tactical, strategic.

Decision scope: extent of the potential impact of a decision
Models of decision making include:

» Rational – managers optimize
» Normative – managers satisfice
» Garbage Can – random alchemy
» Thinking, seeing, doing – science, art, craft
» Decision-making model – five decision styles from autocratic to consensus, matched to decision situations.

NOTES

1 Allison, G.T. (1971), *Essence of Decision: Explaining the Cuban missile crisis*. Little Brown, Boston, Mass.
2 Drummond, H. (1996) *Effective Decision-Making*, 2nd edn. Kogan Page, London.
3 '*Exec*' Home Page, 17 June 1997.
4 Huber, G.P. (1980) *Managerial Decision Making*. Scott, Foresman, Glenview, IL.
5 Kreitner, R. and Kinicki, A. (1995) *Organizational Behavior*, 3rd edn. Richard D. Irwin, Inc., Chicago, IL.
6 Simon, H. (1979) "Rational decision making in business organizations." *The American Economic Review*, September 1979, p. 510, as cited in Kreitner, R. and Kinicki, A. (1995) *Organizational Behavior*, 3rd edn. Richard D. Irwin, Inc., Chicago, IL.
7 Cohen, M., March, J. and Olsen, J. (1989) "A garbage can model of organizational choice." *Administrative Science Quarterly*, June 1989, pp.190–207.

8 Mintzberg, H. and Westley, F. (2001) "It's not what you think." *MIT Sloan Management Review*, Spring 2001.

9 Vroom, V. and Yetton, P. (1973) *Leadership and Decision Making*. University of Pittsburgh Press, Pittsburgh, PA.

10 Vroom, V. and Jago, A. (1988) *The New Leadership: Managing Participation in Organizations*. Prentice-Hall, Englewood Cliffs, NJ.

11 See for example Paul, R.J. and Ebadi, Y.M. "Leadership decision making in a service organization: A field test of the Vroom-Yetton model." *Journal of Occupational and Organizational Psychology*, **62**, 201–211.

The Evolution of Decision Making

Management and the decisions that are its lifeblood have been with us for millennia. In recent years business thinkers have combed ancient texts, even the Bible, for guidance on making business decisions. This chapter briefly traces major historical shifts in approaches to managerial decision making, from aristocracies, to rationality embodied in bureaucracies, and ultimately to the "infocracies" that are emerging in this information age.

» From aristocracies to bureaucracies
» The age of rationality
» The fruits of rationality
» Winds of change
» From bureaucracies to infocracies
» Key learning points

The evolution of managerial decision making may be traced in any number of ways. Historical specimens of outstanding decisions may be ordered by type or chronology. Practices of various cultures may be explored anthropologically. The philosophies and winning formulae of the captains of industry could be investigated. The contributions of various academic disciplines and research might be reviewed. Each is a valid approach, and given the breadth and depth of the topic, each would take a volume to cover in and of itself.

Suffice it to say that, whatever the approach, in the beginning there was management, and along with it the making of managerial decisions that are its lifeblood. This is important to keep in mind in the temporally-centric modern business world where decades of textbooks trace the origins of management to the likes of Frederick Taylor early in the last century. This conveniently ignores the small fact that pyramids, cities, and entire civilizations were built, work distributed, and workers managed in the relentless pursuit of human enterprise, long before the dawn of the twentieth century.

To be clear, these activities have been around in one form or another for at least several millennia. Thus one would have to dig through the pages of history to trace the bulk of the evolution of managerial decision making.

Indeed the broad sweep of history is rich with lessons in managerial decision making. Cultural treasures are increasingly trawled by management writers and thinkers in the hopes of harvesting insights – and best sellers – through the application of managerial lenses. For example, witness the recent stream of books hailing Jesus Christ as a management exemplar (for example, *Jesus CEO*[1] and *The Management Methods of Jesus*,[2] among others).

Even the Old Testament is now viewed as a ready source of management decisions. "By deciding to divide people into their tens, hundreds and thousands, Moses was the first to establish a hierarchy, a chain of command," observes the University of Southern California's Warren Bennis.[3] Think of Noah the project manager making weighty logistical decisions to a tight and immovable deadline. "Could we include Joseph's advice to the Pharaoh on planting wheat to store for seven years?" asked Philip Kotler of Northwestern's Kellogg School when the question of nominating a great management decision was put to him. "Or Jesus' choice of his 12 disciples (except the blunder of Judas)? One could play with the question for years."[4]

The truth is, the more you look to history for management decisions, the more you see. None of the great monuments throughout time would have been created if it weren't for management and frequently fortuitous decision making. The Italian painters of the Renaissance may have been artistic geniuses but they were also shrewd managers able to take advantage of delegation. The teams of laborers who helped build London's St Paul's Cathedral did not gather spontaneously – they were recruited and managed.

FROM ARISTOCRACIES TO BUREAUCRACIES

Business writer James Clawson[5] identifies two major historical shifts that have had a significant impact on power, management, and the way decisions are made. First, male-dominated aristocracies were the prevailing model of governance throughout most of history. Then the Industrial Revolution and accompanying political revolutions in America and France ushered in the age of bureaucracies and democracies. In aristocracies, decision making was the right and responsibility of the ruling family. However, "as the new managerial system took hold, the underlying assumption shifted from 'father knows best' to 'the boss knows best'." This made sense in an age when most workers were uneducated and unskilled, drawn from the farms to work in factories in the rapidly developing cities. Further, lineage in aristocracies made the choice of successor to the king or emperor relatively clear. However, in bureaucracies it was more difficult to determine who the next CEO would be.

The emerging assumption that "the boss knows best" gradually led to the centralization of decision making and power. It also led to hierarchical, functionally differentiated structures. This transition was powerfully influenced by the application of the tools of science to just about everything of any interest to man (and until relatively recently, access to the scientific kingdom was largely limited to men).

THE AGE OF RATIONALITY

Although there have always been managerial – or perhaps magisterial – decisions, decision theory is a decidedly more recent development. And the great bulk of decision theory and the discipline of decision science have been built upon rationality. The great Swiss physicist Daniel Bernoulli first introduced the concept of decision theory in 1738. His theory attempted to explain the non-linear valuation of money. That rational, normative theory was further developed in the 1920s by Frank Ramsey, the British mathematician and philosopher, and in the 1940s by Neumann and Morgenstern, the creators of a set of mathematical theories called the theory of games (extensive research has since been conducted in game theory).

One of the crowning achievements of the twentieth century was the creation of management as a discipline, as a profession, and sometimes as a calling. Early in the last century, Frederick Taylor, an engineer, applied scientific principles to studying the rapidly evolving phenomena of manufacturing organizations. Taylor believed that there was "one best way" to perform a job, and that jobs should be engineered to those specifications. There was no room or need for employee involvement in decision making or innovation.

Perhaps that made sense given the nature of the workforce, rapidly evolving technology, and socio-cultural factors of the time. However, the hallowed objectivity of "true" science is in fact deeply influenced by philosophical perspectives and metaphors. Until quite recently, science was firmly rooted in Newtonian physics, through which the universe is perceived as a machine. This machine model of the universe had (and continues to have) a profound impact on the development and practice of science and management until the waning decades of the twentieth century.

Thus Taylor's "Scientific Management" was in fact mechanistic, rational management. Build and run the organization as a finely-tuned machine. In a machine, the parts – the workers – are interchangeable. The system must be engineered so as to maximize performance and optimize efficiency. System optimization requires top-down management, with strategic decisions made from high up on the corporate throne and operational decisions made by managers perched high above the workers on the factory floor. This enabled the Boss above to see all and consequently know what was best.

The evolution of thinking regarding business decision making during the last century consists of multiple threads from fields of study that developed relatively independently of each other. Each discipline contributes valuable perspectives on the decision-making process, though most had been similarly immersed in the rational worldview (and some still are) until quite recently. Those fields include, but are not limited to:

» economics and statistics, which provide extensive research on utility/value and probability;
» mathematics, which brings models and simulation, key ingredients in decision analysis and support systems;
» psychology, which yields finely textured insights into the behavior of individual decision-makers; and
» social psychology and sociology, which offer guidance on decision processes in groups.

An entire academic discipline, decision science, is devoted to understanding management decision making. Much of it is built on the foundations set down by "early" business thinkers who believed that under a given set of circumstances human behavior was logical and therefore predictable. The fundamental belief of the likes of computer pioneer, Charles Babbage, and Scientific Management founder, Frederick Taylor, was that the decision process (and many other things) could be rationalized and systematized. Based on this premise, emerged models to explain the workings of commerce which, it was thought, could be extended to the way in which decisions were made.

Overall, the story of managerial decision making in the most recent century had essentially been one of deep quasi-religious devotion to a rational ideal anchored in a Newtonian, mechanistic model of the universe. Taylor's Scientific Management was a natural by-product of that worldview, and appropriate for its time, but not ours. Not for knowledge workers in the new age of "infocracies" (see "From bureaucracies to 'infocracies'" below).

THE FRUITS OF RATIONALITY

One of the choicest fruits of rationality and a key outgrowth of decision science has been the development of "decision support systems" (DSS). DSS may be defined as "interactive computer-based systems intended to help decision makers use data and models to identify and solve problems and make decisions."[6] There are many types of DSS, ranging from decision support tools that reside on a desktop computer, to "enterprise-wide systems" that link all managers or users in a firm and beyond (e.g. customers, suppliers) to a massive centralized data warehouse and associated tools for decision analysis and support. These systems may be driven by documents, communications, models, knowledge, and/or data.

Decision support systems are rapidly infiltrating our daily lives, even if we're not aware that we're using them (which is, of course, the ideal). For example, if you use a word processing software program like MS Word, you've probably used a basic and rather helpful form of DSS – the spelling and grammar check. The program facilitates and expedites proofreading functions by searching documents for potential errors in categories ranging from spelling and punctuation to word choice and grammar. It also provides users with instant access to a variety of choices for errors it identifies, along with background information to support the user in making decisions regarding those choices. Of course these tools have their limitations, as you've probably experienced. Even so, we've rapidly come to rely on them, and this is but one among many possible examples of commonly used DSS.

In case you're worried that a slick new DSS might actually replace you, relax. The good and the bad news is that DSS won't make decisions for you (at least not yet!). That's been a common misunderstanding about DSS. "The thrust of decision support for the past 30 years has been to realize that computers are tools, adjuncts to decision making," says Daniel J. Power, Professor of Information Systems at the University of Northern Iowa, editor of DSSResources.COM, and a leading expert on DSS. "Computers are there to assist in information retrieval and application of analytical tools to data, to do the things that computers do best. We try to present the information in a way that allows people to make better decisions, but not to have the computer make decisions for people.

"There are certainly computerized systems that make decisions – we have them in manufacturing and power plants, for example – but that's not what DSS is all about. It's about supporting a manager in making decisions as part of a business process. To make fact-based decisions in an organization – monitoring and controlling activities or planning. The idea has never been that the software was going to make decisions for managers."

It's important to keep in mind that every step in designing and programming a DSS involves making complex decisions that will determine its ultimate utility. It is deeply entrenched in a mechanistic model of the universe through which it is assumed that thought processes may be scientifically diced and sliced into manageable bits that may be arranged in rational sequence. While this perspective serves us well in many, many ways, it still cannot deal with the vagaries of human emotions like the paralyzing fear that might prevent someone from going through with a recommended procedure (e.g. surgical option) no matter how highly they may rank it on other dimensions.

This is why they are called decision *support* systems. They cannot make difficult decisions for us (although recurring, routine decisions are definitely being made automatically via DSS applications in a variety of settings), but only suggest "optimal" choices – and this is key – *based upon the quality and comprehensiveness of the questions asked, analyses performed, and data provided*. Primary challenges involve identifying all of the critical questions that pertain to the particular topic and determining how to weight responses in a way that is relevant for the user. It's easy to lose sight of these issues in the flash of marketing surrounding DSS products and their success stories, which are truly impressive, but we should always keep these basic issues in mind when considering the use of DSS.

Another drawback to reliance upon any decision-making model or DSS is that identifying what you need to make a decision about is often more important than the actual decision itself. If a decision seeks to solve a problem, it may be the right decision but the wrong problem. The reality is that managers make decisions based on a combination of intuition, experience, and analysis, as recent research demonstrates.[7]

As intuition and experience are impossible to measure in any sensible way, the temptation is to focus on the analytical side of decision making, the science rather than the craft or mysterious art. (The great bulk of the management consultancy industry is based on reaching decisions through rational analysis.) Of course, the manager in the real world does not care whether he or she is practicing an art or science. What they do care about is solving problems and reaching reliable, well-informed decisions.

DSS is discussed more fully in Chapter 4, and a success story using DSS is offered in Chapter 7.

WINDS OF CHANGE

The achievements of rationality notwithstanding, the last quarter century has witnessed a quickening struggle to break free of the rational stronghold. Herbert Simon challenged rational decision-making dogma in 1978[8] and won the Nobel Prize. Thomas Peters and Robert Waterman, Jr. devoted an entire chapter to unraveling the rational model in their landmark 1982 book, *In Search of Excellence*.[9] In his 1994 book, *The Rise and Fall of Strategic Planning*,[10] management scholar Henry Mintzberg challenged the rational approach to strategic planning. To be fair, it was *research and thinking* regarding decision making that was enslaved to the rationalistic model, but this deeply influenced practice, as well as social mores concerning what could legitimately be discussed within the realm of management and decision making.

What Simon, Mintzberg, Peters, and Waterman, among others, began to discover and – more importantly – widely communicate, was that real life managerial decisions were forged out of a complex mix of rationality, emotionality, intuition, experience, chance, and other factors. Contrary to common belief, those decisions could not be adequately represented or modeled with decision analysis and decision trees, no matter how complex and well designed they might be. Not all would agree however, and even today millions maintain their devotion to the pure rationalistic ideal.

Significant shifts in worldview take considerable time however – Internet revolution notwithstanding – and countless institutions forged their reputations and developed their programs in support of rational management. To be sure, power is at stake here. Professional associations, academic institutions – including the "top tier" journals – had a vested interest in perpetuating their traditional power bases, which are of course rooted in the religion of rationality – and the funding that copiously flows from its wealthy corporate and government adherents. Even though forays into the "non-rational" (e.g. intuition) are now considered, they typically must meet rationalistic criteria in order to be granted a place at the management science banquet table.

This is not to say that rationality should be discarded or overthrown. Rational approaches to management and decision making are an essential *part* of the mix. However, they are a part, not the whole. The failure rates of managerial decisions and DSS implementations discussed in Chapters 1 and 4 suggest that blind adherence to rational problem-solving approaches to decision making may never get us to where we'd like to be – which is something better than a coin toss, for sure.

Fortunately, winds of change are afoot, and have been for quite some time. The evidence for substantive change is everywhere, though set in stark relief against the backdrop of rationality's continued deep entrenchment.

FROM BUREAUCRACIES TO "INFOCRACIES"

During the past half century, another transition has been taking place. As far back as 1960, management visionary Warren Bennis predicted that bureaucracies were dying. He predicted that the "ponderous decision making and functional divisions of the Industrial Age bureaucracy would render them obsolete."[11] Stable industry environments were increasingly plowed under by the accelerating churn of technological change, and autocratic "boss knows best" decision making gradually gave way to greater employee involvement in significant organizational decision processes. The workforce became highly educated, natural and manufacturing resources became commoditized, and information rose to primacy as the key resource at the center of organizational life.

We are now immersed in the information age, and James Clawson identifies the second major historical shift as being from bureaucracy to "infocracy." In a bureaucracy, power and authority are vested in offices/positions, not individuals. Laws and policies take precedence over the personal judgment associated with aristocracy. In an infocracy, data is at the core, and it overrides both policies and personal judgment. Authority is vested in those who interpret the data. The implication is that decisions are data-driven, or at least data-justified. As Clawson explains, power "migrates to whomever is closest to the key challenges facing the organization at any given time and who has access to the relevant data for making the appropriate decision."[12] Thus decision making is seen as being data-based and highly distributed to nodes of interpretive expertise throughout the organization.

This may be a good thing. It certainly sounds like the crowning achievement of rationality. However, as discussed above and in Chapter 6, access to data and decision analysis tools, no matter how sophisticated, are necessary but insufficient conditions for effective managerial decision making in the twenty-first century. They take us to the edges of rationality, the places that require engagement of the whole manager, not just the rational analyst. These are the places where the art and craft of decision making – drawing upon other forms of data, including one's intuition, insight, foresight, gut feelings, and spiritual and moral fortitude – separate the coin-flippers from the pros.

KEY LEARNING POINTS

» Managerial decisions were made long before the dawn of the twentieth century.
» Two key historical shifts:
  » from aristocracies to bureaucracies
  » from bureaucracies to infocracies.
» Rational management, rooted in a machine model of the universe, dominated the twentieth century.
» Decision support systems are one of the crowning achievements of decision science.
» The limits to rational decision making have been increasingly challenged in the last quarter century.
» Rationality is an important *part* of decision making, but not the whole.
» Managerial decision making is as much art and craft as it is science.

NOTES

1 Jones, L.B. (1996) *Jesus CEO: Using Ancient Wisdom for Visionary Leadership*. Hyperion, New York.

2 Briner, B. (1996) *The Management Methods of Jesus: Ancient Wisdom for Modern Business*. Thomas Nelson, 1996.

3 Interview with Des Dearlove.

4 Correspondence with Des Dearlove.

5 Clawson, J. (2000) "The new infocracies: Implications for leadership." Ivey Business Journal, London, May/June 2000.

6 Power, D.J., (2001) *Decision Support Systems Web Tour*. http://dssresources.com/tour, version 4.1, 3 March, 2001.

7 Khatri, N. and Ng, A.H. (2000) "The role of intuition in strategic decision-making." *Human Relations*, January 2000.

8 Simon, H. (1979) "Rational decision making in business organizations." *The American Economic Review*, September 1979, p. 510, as cited in Kreitner, R. and Kinicki, A. (1995) *Organizational Behavior*, 3rd edn. Richard D. Irwin, Inc., Chicago, IL.

9 Peters, T.J. and Waterman, R.H. Jr. (1982) *In Search of Excellence*. Warner Books, New York.

10 Mintzberg, H. (1994) *The Rise and Fall of Strategic Planning*. Free Press, New York.

11 Author interview.

12 Clawson, J., *ibid*.

The E-Dimension

The Internet is having a profound and pervasive impact on managerial decision making. The reputation of decision-support systems had been tarnished in the decade prior to the Internet, and DSS implementations suffer from unacceptably high failure rates. There is a resurgence of interest and massive corporate investment in DSS, however, thanks to the possibilities that the Internet and intranets provide. But will this massive investment really help managers make more effective decisions?

» Group decision support systems
» Reducing high failure rates in DSS implementations
» Best practice: The Valio Group
» Brave new future?
» Key learning points

The "e-dimension" has revolutionized – or at the very least significantly infiltrated – every aspect of modern life, including business decision making. The ubiquity of electronic exchange systems and media is supporting efforts to drive organizational decision making down to the frontline by giving an ever greater range of personnel instant access to information and decision support tools. These tools range from data warehouses and enterprise-wide DSS, to systems that support collaborative decision making in geographically dispersed virtual teams.

Dr J.D. Eveland is a knowledge management professional and organizational research specialist with over 20 years' experience in business, government, and academic institutions, including 15 years as a senior consultant to the RAND Corporation (www.jdeveland.com). According to Eveland, "the main thing that's changed is the move into the Internet environment and the greater degree of connectivity. The decision support systems that operated in the eighties and early nineties were dedicated systems – you couldn't access them except by dialing into them. The difference now is that since virtually everything operates in the Internet environment, you can access anything through a variety of means. We're almost too connected in this respect. What you now have is the pervasiveness of access to the technology. The Internet has not changed technology in this area, it has changed access to the technology, and by changing that you have changed most of the things about the ways that organizations use it."

Not all managers are eager to embark on brave new DSS implementations, however. Some who lived through the wide-eyed enthusiasm for the possibilities of DSS in the eighties remain reluctant to jump on the recently revived DSS bandwagon. Daniel J. Power, a leading expert on DSS, offers some historical perspective. "The introduction of the personal computer in the early eighties gave people the impression that technologies had reached the level that we could do just about anything in terms of providing support to managers. By about 1986–87, managers became somewhat disillusioned with the capabilities and promises that vendors and information systems staffs made about the systems that they were going to put into place.

"In the early nineties there was a slowdown and a waiting period as graphical user interfaces like Windows 3.1 were introduced and new software were developed for that platform. The introduction of data warehouses, some of the analytical processing tools, and what I call data-driven decision-support systems opened up new possibilities for providing enterprise-wide DSS for managers. I think it's all really taken off since the Web and the Internet reinvigorated some of the tech firms and forced them to move their software onto a new platform. That's all happened in the last five years."

The speed and pervasiveness of this revolution have been breath-taking. As Eveland points out, "what's truly amazing is how fast this has moved from "what's an Internet?" to, "oh, the Internet." Think back – it's only been four or five years really. The first use of the term "Internet" was less than 10 years ago, which is utterly bizarre when you realize that it's now pervasive in our lives. This is one of the most rapid and dramatic social changes that has ever taken place. There's been nothing like it in history in terms of the combination of pervasiveness and the rapidity of the change, and we're just beginning to feel what it is all about."

GROUP DECISION SUPPORT SYSTEMS (GDSS)

GDSS are but one form of decision support systems that are being transformed by the e-dimension. The need for Web-based GDSS has skyrocketed with the onslaught of geographically dispersed virtual teams, and the Web is radically changing the ways in which people interact with these systems. "One of the things that the Internet does is transfer control of the interface from the specialist to the user," says J.D. Eveland, "and in the Internet environment, it is the user that can manipulate and control the environment, rather than waiting for the expert to run the system for them. In the 'old' days, the control of the GDSS was entirely in the hands of the facilitator, the manipulator, who was essentially the interface with the technology. Everything was in the hands of the techie who ran the GDSS, and you were acutely aware that your interaction with the system was being managed through a technical specialist. What that does is distance you from the technology – the tool is something that you are acutely aware of, because there is something standing between you and it.

"What these new interfaces have done is give people a sense of personal control over their tools," Eveland notes, "so that the barriers between them and their tools becomes less. And the lower the barriers between the individuals and the system, the more the system becomes a part of the group, rather than something outside of ourselves that we have to deal with.''

Just in case you hadn't noticed, computers have rapidly become an integral part of many groups. ''The idea of having a conversation with a computer was so outrageously bizarre back in 1971 when *2001: A Space Odyssey* came out, to regard a machine as a person, we now have reached that point, and we've reached it without even being aware of it,'' Eveland marvels. ''But the barriers are so much less that the tool becomes a part of the group and the information it provides is regarded as the same as the information provided by somebody else. So what we're dealing with is the lowering of the boundaries if you will between people and their technology.''

REDUCING HIGH FAILURE RATES IN DSS IMPLEMENTATIONS

Although the Web has transformed the possibilities for DSS, it unfortunately hasn't increased the effectiveness of DSS implementations. For example, ''40 or 50 or 60% of data warehouse implementations are failures by one or more measures,'' laments Dan Power. Of course, these failure rates are in the same ballpark as those observed in recent years across a broad spectrum of executive decisions.[1] Nevertheless, Dan believes that ''we should expect that these systems are going to succeed more than they fail. I'm not going to say that it should be 100% in big data or model driven systems, but I think that we should be getting 70–75% success rates rather than the numbers I see out there in various studies.''

Not surprisingly, people issues tend to be responsible for more system failures than technology issues, according to Dan Power. ''The technology may have done what it was intended to do, but the failure rate is higher because people got frustrated with the system,'' says Dan. Thus the level of attention paid to people issues can make or break the chances for success when implementing a sophisticated DSS.

There are some ways that managers can improve the likelihood of a successful DSS implementation, however. Dr Don Mankin, author of *Teams & Technology*,[2] argues ''user involvement is probably the most critical factor. It's important to get users involved early on in a meaningful way, with ongoing involvement. They need to be participants in the major decisions. You can't just ask them one time what they want and then go ahead and make decisions and feed it back to them later on. So ongoing involvement is probably the critical feature.

"A second critical feature is having an open-ended change process. You can't predict what the outcomes of the implementation process are going to be. Don't be too rigid about your expectations. Be open about the results of the process, and keep the process flexible so that you can make mid-course corrections."

Today, most firms will have no difficulty finding a DSS that fits – or that may be customized to fit – their particular needs, but the cost-effectiveness of a system is a critical issue that also needs to be addressed early on. "Some decisions don't justify large investments in computing technology," advises Dan Power. "The challenge is to figure out which application will yield the highest return in the short run. And I'm not sure that building more data warehouse systems is going to be the way for most firms to go. It's easy for such large, complex systems to go unused because managers don't know what they can do with them, and they are very expensive to create."

Thus the needs and preferences of those who will be using the system need to be considered from the very beginning. Unfortunately, it's both common and "easy to neglect the issues of what kind of a system managers want to use and will use," according to Power. "A system is often added to an existing process, rather than looking at what the tasks really are that we need to perform, and what the role of a DSS could be. I still think most of our systems are developed in isolation. I don't think that when analysts consider systems that they look at how they will be used. Typically there's a project sponsor that's heard that a competitor has implemented a DSS system, and that's the starting point, rather than beginning from the standpoint of organizational decisions and decision processes." That's an example of the most common and least effective tactic that managers use to impose direction in decision-making processes – latch onto an available idea and quickly transform it into a ready-made "solution."[3]

In order to counteract these tendencies, "companies should do a decision-process audit of how decisions are made in the company now," Dan Power advises. "A lot of this is still about thinking. Decision support is a lot about thinking and analysis – looking for opportunities to put DSS into an organization is a major cognitive task. Start by finding someone smart to help you look at your organization. I think a number of consulting firms would say that they start by looking at processes and existing decision systems in organizations. In my book[4] I've put together some steps to take in a decision-audit and some audit questions that managers can ask themselves about their knowledge of decision support and how it occurs in their organization."

BEST PRACTICE: THE VALIO GROUP, FINLAND'S LARGEST DAIRY COMPANY[5]

The Valio Group is a nearly 100-year-old cooperative of Finnish farmers that supplies 70% of Finland's fresh milk. With annual revenues in excess of $1.6bn, Valio is not only Finland's largest dairy company, but also its second largest food company by net sales. From the produce of 38 Finnish dairies, it generates 800 food products that it distributes to 60 countries.

Valio faces new challenges in the twenty-first century. For example, Finland's entry into the European Union has resulted in heightened competition, and Russia's economic woes have negatively impacted sales in a region that is strategically important for Valio. To cope with these and other demands, and to thrive in a dynamic global industry ripe with opportunities as well as threats, Valio streamlined and integrated its supply chain – from dairies to distribution centers – and built a knowledge management environment that gives it access to the accurate, up-to-the minute information that it needs to support effective decision making throughout the organization.

Thanks to Valio's huge market share, it was able to build a larger and more sophisticated data warehouse than its competitors, according to Peter Bretag, Valio IT manager. The massive warehouse, based on a highly available platform provided by Compaq and Oracle, integrates data across all of Valio's 30 corporate applications. It is a transaction-intensive environment that tracks information on more than 3 million sales a month. Better still, it enables Valio to accommodate the needs of both internal and external users in its supply chain through a single, dynamic system.

Valio decision-makers now have easy access to consistent, timely, and accurate information and analysis capabilities via the Web. "Senior decision makers enjoy easy-to-use World Wide Web-based access to warehouse data," says Bretag. In fact, one key to the system's successful implementation has been its ease of use. For example, Bretag observes, "even executives who are new to PCs use the system with no training. The summaries enable managers to respond quickly to business developments based on up-to-the-minute information. Further, they have the tools to drill down for more in-depth analyses."

Building on its existing online customer ordering capacity via an extranet, Valio plans to offer wholesalers an extranet-based data mart that will contain in-house and third party market data as well as raw materials forecasts. Sharing such information, Valio and its buyers will be able to adapt order flows and production schedules to consumer buying patterns. This collaboration will enable Valio and its customers to hone a more competitive supply chain and strengthen consumer loyalty to Valio brands.

In the dairy business, Valio is certainly the cream that rises to the top. While others merely graze the market's potential, Valio uses data warehouse technology to unlock opportunities its competitors miss. As an innovative technology adopter, Valio provides an outstanding benchmark for companies that seek to leverage information assets, cut costs, and increase revenues through successful implementation of data warehousing via the Web.

Benefits of data warehouse to Valio

» Easy, ubiquitous access to vast market intelligence.
» Faster response to dynamic business trends.
» Consumer-centric supply chain.
» Shorter time-to-market with innovation.
» Sophisticated system but low cost of ownership.

BRAVE NEW FUTURE?

Given the impact of the e-dimension on DSS in just a few short years, what might the future have in store? Dan Power thinks that "ten years from now managers are going to be better-informed decision makers than they've ever been. They're going to have access to facts – whether they're smart enough to use that information wisely is still going to be a concern. The computer is just a tool, DSS is just a tool – like a hammer, you can still hit your finger with it. And there will be some people who use it inappropriately, and some people who can't hit a nail to save their lives. But I'm very optimistic that we'll start to see a transformation in decision making as we have in the operations area. Technology integration will continue to happen because our population keeps increasing and demands for goods and services keeps increasing. The only way we can meet that demand is not just by using transaction-processing systems, but also decision support systems."

But progress does not guarantee perfection. J.D. Eveland notes that "we're moving toward ever easier interfaces, a greater ability to interact with the machines, and a greater ability of the machines to gather information. There are multiple ways in which it can move, and we can move in all of them simultaneously – better information, better incorporation of the information into DSS, and better decisions, as well as more information, more confusion, and worse decisions."

So what then, is the answer? Are we at the dawn of a glorious new age in which more and more managers will bask in the afterglow of their decision-making prowess, enhanced by sophisticated Web-based DSS? Not likely. "Look, we've got some of the smartest people in the world running the Fortune 500," Eveland says. "At any given moment half of them are doing O.K., and half of them are going downhill. And the fact is that the half that are going downhill are run by people who are just as smart as the ones that are running the ones that are going uphill. Smarts has its limits. We are living in a world system that is so complicated that only small pieces of it can be comprehended and manipulated by smarts, and that's smarts by machines as well as by people. We're continuing to expand the boundaries of what machines mean by smart. We're also continually expanding the bounds of what's required to make the systems work. And the fact that the machines are getting smarter is paralleled by the difficulties of making the systems work. So I don't know what the answer is. The fact is, we're making the world both more difficult and easier simultaneously, and neither of them is guaranteed either way."

Coin toss, anyone?

KEY LEARNING POINTS

» The Internet has revolutionized business decision making.
» Group decision support systems are one form of DSS that have been transformed by the Internet.
» Reduce high failure rates of DSS implementations by:
  » involving users in a meaningful way;
  » having an open-ended change process; and
  » doing a decision-process audit.
» Technological advances do not guarantee decision-making effectiveness.

NOTES

1 Nutt, P. (1999) "Surprising but true: Half the decisions in organizations fail." *Academy of Management Executive* **13**(4).
2 Mankin, D., Cohen, S. and Bikson, T. (1996) *Teams & Technology – Fulfilling the Promise of the New Organization.* Harvard Business School Press, Boston, MA.
3 Nutt, P., *ibid.*
4 Power, D. (in press) *Decision Support Systems: An Expanded Framework* (working title). Greenwood Publishing Group, Quorum Books (www.quorumbooks.com).
5 Peter Bretag, IT manager, The Valio Group, Helsinki, Finland, commenting in *Data Warehousing: What Works?*™ Volume 9, April 2000.

The Global Dimension

No business is immune from the pervasive influence of globalization. This chapter addresses the complex challenges associated with implementing DSS on a global basis, and with cultural differences in approaches to decision making. A "cultural prism" may be used to help managers better understand their own culture as well as other cultures in which they make decisions.

» Complexity in DSS
» Cultural diversity in decision making
» Global manager's perspective
» Appreciating culture
» Key learning points

Globalization is having a profound impact on all aspects of business and all types of companies, from global corporations to "local" manufacturers. That impact is interwoven with that of the e-dimension to simultaneously create powerful opportunities and threats. In fact, the global and e-dimensions are so inextricably interlinked that it can be difficult to separate one from the other. For example, a small manufacturer of dishes for institutional use in the mid-Western US had a dependable customer base in its region for several decades. A primary customer was a very large hospital system in that region. One day a purchaser for the hospital went online and found a comparable product offering at a cheaper price available through a manufacturer in Eastern Europe, and that led to the swift downfall of the US manufacturer. While perhaps there will always remain some businesses that are truly local and relatively unaffected by globalization, the brief story above illustrates the impact of the global, Web-linked economy on businesses large and small, no matter where they may be.

A business now competes not only with comparable products and services offered by other companies in its region, country, and continent, but potentially from anywhere in the world. This opens up vast new markets and greatly increases the challenges and opportunities for all concerned. The manufacturer in Eastern Europe reaches a buyer deep in the US heartland, the purchaser for the hospital has a cornucopia of global product offerings from which to choose, as well as greatly expanded opportunities to reduce costs and/or increase quality by changing suppliers. Meanwhile the manufacturer that still conceives of itself as a "local" business may get trampled in the dust of the global gold rush. And all of this impacts managerial decision making. It influences everything from routine day-to-day decisions to long-range planning.

COMPLEXITY IN DECISION-SUPPORT SYSTEMS

Globalization is not only intricately intertwined with the e-dimension, it is having a significant impact on it. One example is in designing and implementing support systems for global decision making. Don Mankin, author of *Teams & Technology*,[1] says that that impact "is really one of complexity. The further the reach of the system, the greater the number of users that will be impacted. What does user involvement mean when you are talking about a system with global reach? You're not just talking about increased numbers of users, but users that may be very different in terms of the cultures that they come from and the ways in which they use and relate to technology."[2]

The impact of diverse user needs is complex enough when thinking in terms of global DSS within a single organization. That complexity escalates when decisions need to be integrated across multiple organizations in multiple countries and cultures. "For example, with these Internet-based enterprise systems you are crossing cultural and organizational boundaries," Mankin says. "The kind of thing that SAP and Oracle sell – supply chain systems that companies use to try to integrate manufacturing or services across the supply chain, where you have different suppliers, manufacturers, and distributors that all need to be integrated, and you need a common information system and metrics that will integrate all of them. This is probably the highest level of complexity that you can find, because not only do you have different companies that may be located in different regions and time zones, but also different nations."

The challenge of making business decisions in massive, transorganizational projects is mind-boggling. "The Boeing 777 project was an international project of this order," Mankin notes. "It was a massive project, probably the largest commercial project in our history. And it was a successful project. They built a DSS (a CAD system) specifically to support it and the multiple project teams that were scattered around the world working on it. I believe that they built the system essentially from scratch. It was a multi-billion dollar project, so they had the luxury of asking themselves what kind of system ideally would meet their needs. They then developed decision protocols for the project, so that the way that decisions were made was standardized. They developed a decision system and process that would lead people in a very systematic way to the decision they needed.

"Under normal circumstances a team gets together and makes a decision. Well in this case you're talking about a complex design task involving people all over the world that didn't even know each other except through this project, and that rarely met face-to-face. So it was not the case of people getting together and throwing out ideas, the amount of structuring beforehand was much greater. In simpler projects you can afford to have things be more spontaneous, but you need to provide much more structure up front in complex projects. But then the risk is that you structure things so much that you lose creativity and innovation. So you want to have just enough structure so that things don't collapse into chaos, but you don't want to have so much structure that you suppress creativity, innovation, and spontaneity.''

Unfortunately, most companies don't have the multi-billion dollar luxury of building their own system to support global decision making from scratch. But the Boeing case illustrates the challenges and possibilities of integrating business decisions in global alliances. Given the rapid proliferation of such alliances and networks, the ability to effectively support global decision processes across organizations and cultures is vitally important.

CULTURAL DIVERSITY IN DECISION MAKING

One aspect of the global dimension that is amplified by the Internet but which predates it and exists independently of it is the interplay of cultures and the diversity of their respective decision-making styles and processes. The tectonic plates of individualistic and collectivistic, free-market and formerly controlled economic cultures shift and collide against one another as organizations race headlong into the global economy. This creates opportunities to experience and experiment with different approaches to decision making in order to enrich our repertoire. However, it may also lead to inefficiency, misunderstanding, and conflict as people from each culture engage in decision processes from the vantage of their own cultural practices.

For example, a process known as ''Ringi'' is used in decision making by Japanese companies. Proposals circulate within the organization and are initialed by agreeing participants. Most critical of all, it eliminates the need to ''sell'' the decision later. As such, it actually builds effective implementation into the decision-making process. It is probably the best-known example of collectivist decision making.

It differs markedly, however, from typical American approaches. To illustrate the difference, Peter Drucker offers the example of a US executive negotiating a license agreement with a Japanese executive.[3] The Westerner finds it difficult to understand why the Japanese executive keeps sending new groups of people who start what the Westerner thinks are negotiations as if they know nothing about what has been discussed before. One delegation is succeeded six weeks later by another team from another part of the company who proceed as if they know nothing of what has gone before.

As Drucker explains, this is actually a sign that the Japanese take the matter seriously. They are trying to involve the people who will eventually have to put the agreement into practice. The aim is to obtain consensus that a license is indeed needed. Only when all of these people have reached agreement on the need to make a decision will the decision be made to go ahead. It is only at this stage that the real negotiations start – and then the Japanese usually move with great speed.

By the time the "decision" or action is finally agreed it will come as no surprise to the organization, and will meet little or no resistance. As a result, implementation is much faster. As a result of his observations, Drucker concluded that the difficulty of selling decisions to others is the chief reason for their failure in US companies. Sound familiar? Paul Nutt's research – two decades later – came to similar conclusions: 50% of the decision implementations that he observed in US and Canadian organizations failed.[4] Clearly, building fast, effective implementation into the decision-making process is vitally important.

Fine, then you say, why don't Western companies just adopt the Japanese model? If only it were that simple, but of course things rarely are. The truth is that the Japanese decision-making process or model is specific to that culture. It relies on the cultural understandings and social systems that together make up the organization.

For one thing, most Western cultures are based on the principle of "individualism" to a much greater extent than Eastern cultures. It would be untrue to say that the Japanese culture is based entirely on "collectivism," especially today when Western influences are significant, or that American culture is entirely individualistic given the integration of millions of people from collectivist cultures into American society, yet that remains a very significant distinction between the two cultures.

Apart from that, there are also some problems with the Japanese model of decision making. For one thing, as indicated earlier, it is an extremely effective way of reaching a consensus on big decisions. But it is slow and cumbersome for making small or urgent decisions. (This, of course, can be seen as one of the great strengths of the Japanese model – that it encourages "big decisions," which in turn encourages companies to take a long term view.)

What the Japanese method of decision making does teach us is that different national cultures have different ways of approaching decisions. This is something managers ignore at their peril.

GLOBAL MANAGER'S PERSPECTIVE

Brian Hsieh is senior vice president and general manager for Mitsubishi's Electronic Technology Division in Taiwan. He is an electrical engineer with extensive experience in information technology and telecommunications. Brian says, "I've worked for more than three years in a Japanese company, and about eight years in an American company, as well as in Taiwanese companies, so I have some personal experience working with the decision-making styles of three different cultures."

"The Taiwanese personality is quite different from the American, but the management system is very similar. The scale of the Taiwanese company is very small. Small- to medium-sized enterprises comprise about 90% of Taiwanese companies. But you may have to separate Taiwanese companies into three kinds of management systems. The first kind copies the Japanese. The second copies the American style. And the third style, the Taiwanese style, is that the boss can handle all decisions. This may be possible because of the size of the enterprises.

"In my experience, the American style and Taiwanese style of the making and timing of decisions is more flexible. The Japanese style is very serious and more conservative. It takes much time and needs teamwork to reach consensus to make decisions.

"For example, the first time I joined Mitsubishi I thought the Japanese were inefficient. It seemed like it should be very easy to make a decision, and I didn't understand why it took so long to make decisions. But now I think there may be some advantage to their process because during the process everyone expresses their opinions, but commonality is discovered through the process in order to reach the decision. It fosters a harmonious environment.

Second, maybe the decision will be a better decision – maybe not the best decision, but better than the average or normal standard. And third, the decision is really workable with less resistance from other departments or division heads. So potential conflict between departments and divisions is avoided or decreased.

"Interdepartmental conflict is very common in Taiwanese and American companies, but in Japanese companies, you may not see this type of conflict happen. That may be a result of their approach to decision making."

Thus the Ringi process supports not only swift, effective implementation through consensual decision making, but also the development of harmonious interdepartmental relationships. The time invested in the lengthy process may in fact be less costly in the long run than the costs associated with failed implementations and infighting.

APPRECIATING CULTURE

Ideally, the interplay of cultures can enrich our decision-making repertoire and effectiveness. It certainly increases the challenges and opportunities. It can also help us to understand and appreciate not only the decision-making styles of people from other cultures that we work with, but of our own cultural style as well, as it did for Brian Hsieh. In this era of global business, the stakes are increasingly high. Terry Brake, author of *The Global Leader* and president of the management and human resource consultancy TMA-USA, has written extensively on the way cultural differences can affect decision making.[5] He notes that "a clash of cultures affects the bottom line directly and can destroy a potentially rewarding joint venture or strategic alliance." The history of global business is rife with examples of such culture clashes.

In his book, Brake offers a social and psychological "culture prism" as a tool to help managers understand and appreciate other national cultures. Each major group within the culture prism can be broken down into different pairs or triads of cultural preferences. Below is a brief description of how one element – communication – may be viewed through the culture prism.

DIFFERENCES IN CULTURAL COMMUNICATION STYLES

» *Implied*: Meaning lies beneath the surface. Stresses empathy and shared understandings.
» *Stated*: Meaning lies on the surface. Everything is expressed explicitly.
» *Circular*: Maximum explanation of context.
» *Straight*: Minimum explanation of context.
» *Ordered*: Each situation has certain protocols that need to be followed, e.g. people do not speak out of turn.
» *Casual*: Every situation is much like any other. Protocols get in the way of individual expression and honest communication.

The other elements break down in a similar way. Taken together, the elements of the cultural prism can be used as a framework to help understand a particular culture and its possible interplay with another. For example, returning for a moment to the example of the Japanese and the Americans, Brake notes that "in Japan communication tends to be implied rather than stated. 'We stress shared understandings and empathy. We don't need to explain everything because we assume others will understand even before we finish speaking.' This type of communication is common in cultures that stress the importance of group harmony and homogeneity over the individual. Indirect communication helps preserve surface harmony and avoid embarrassment."

Blake goes on to illustrate the Japanese style as being circular and highly ordered. The Ringi process, with its circulation of decision proposals laterally and vertically throughout the organization, is but one example of the Japanese style. The Japanese go to great lengths to provide the full context for the focal decision or issue so that the listener will have a complete picture of the situation. Blake notes that this approach is also typical of Latin American and Southern European countries. In addition, "in Japan communication is very ordered," Blake says. "Each social situation has certain protocols that need to be followed; otherwise there will be confusion and misunderstanding."

In contrast, American communication tends to be directly and casually stated with little context provided. For example, Americans will often begin a presentation or proposal by talking about the bottom line, and provide relatively little context for it. The highly individualistic Americans (and Australians) prefer to bypass communication protocols – which are a hallmark of highly ordered Japanese communication – because they see protocols as obstructions to individual expression and "real, honest" communication. Thus, as the culture prism demonstrates, communication between Japanese and American managers is fraught with potential dangers.

Fortunately, by using Blake's cultural prism as a starting point, managers can better understand their own culture as well as others in which they make decisions. However, the prism is only a tool – one among many – and useful though it may be, Blake notes that "ultimately it is only through reflection on our experiences and a deep respect – a sense of wonder, in fact – for other cultures that we can appreciate the miraculous diversity of the human race." Such respect and appreciation goes a *long* way in successfully navigating the challenging waters of effective decision making in our rapidly globalizing world.

KEY LEARNING POINTS

» Globalization is having a profound impact on business decision making.
» There's no longer any such thing as a "local" company.
» This makes DSS design and implementation extremely complex, especially in global, trans-organizational projects
» Cultural differences in approaches to decision making may lead to conflicts.
» Interplay of cultures can enrich decision-making repertoire.
» Use the "culture prism" as a tool in understanding cultural differences.

NOTES

1 Mankin, D., Cohen, S. and Bikson, T. (1996) *Teams & Technology*. Harvard Business School Press, Boston, MA.

2 Interview with Don Mankin.
3 Drucker, P. (1979) *Management*. Penguin, Harmondsworth.
4 Nutt, P. (1999) "Surprising but true: Half the decisions in organizations fail." *Academy of Management Executive* **13**(4).
5 Brake, T. (1997) *The Global Leader*. Irwin, Burr Ridge, IL.

The State of the Art

The current state of the art in business decision making is multi-faceted. It begins with the development and implementation of systems that provide ubiquitous access to large volumes of accurate and up-to-the-minute information. However, such access is a necessary but insufficient condition for effective decision making. Intuition and contemplative spiritual practice are essential complements to rational approaches, and global social concerns and values are being integrated into every aspect of business decisions. Finally, whole system appreciative approaches engender new vistas of possibilities, far beyond the realm of traditional problem-solving methods.

» State of the rational art of decision making
» Complementing rationality with intuition
» A spiritual compass for decision making
» A global compass for managerial decision making
» Beyond problem solving
» Key learning points

In this chapter we will explore the multi-faceted nature of the "state of the art" in making business decisions in the twenty-first century. We'll begin by honoring the leading edge of the rational tradition as exemplified through decision analysis, modeling, and support in the healthcare industry. Next we'll consider the role of intuition in decision making, and recent research regarding its use by managers. We'll then deepen that exploration by journeying farther inward, to the vital role of spiritual reflection and contemplation in effective decision making.

From this point we'll turn outward, beyond the individual manager, and beyond the manager's individual organization, to the rapidly expanding role of global templates as guides to decision making for organizations that positively contribute to a productive, sustainable future for us all. Thus in the process we'll be exploring three forms of DSS: computer-aided, Web-based; internal, manager-based; and external, global-standards based. Finally, we will venture beyond the realm of the problem-identification-analysis-solution approach in which virtually all decision making has been immersed – even those approaches that transcend the rational – to a systemic, collaborative approach to decision making based on research and experience into the generative capacity of a positively appreciative worldview.

STATE OF THE RATIONAL ART OF DECISION MAKING

Rational approaches to decision making rely upon analysis of massive amounts of information. Of course, "good information does not guarantee good decisions," notes J.D. Eveland, "but bad information pretty much guarantees bad decisions, except by chance. You can have the worst information in the world and by some process of chance you may come across the right decision."[1] Easy access to accurate, timely information is becoming ever more critical. As Eveland implies, however, high quality information is a necessary but insufficient condition for effective decision making.

Further, the rapid shift to infocratic forms of organization (discussed in Chapter 3) places information at the center of organization. And organizational boundaries continue to blur as alliances and networks cluster around common sets of needs – including information. The scope of information required by various stakeholders in such an infocratic alliance becomes increasingly broad, deep, and complex.

Trends in the healthcare industry illustrate these concepts. Morris Raker, co-founder of TreeAge Software (www.treeage.com),[2] a key provider of DSS for the healthcare industry, explains: "Today virtually all medical facilities have what they call treatment guidelines or pathways. What most of these organizations are trying to do is to standardize care – to maintain a high level of care, but avoid people making the wrong decisions. So they have these paper rules that say if your patient has this, do this, etc. But there are a number of problems with this type of system. One of the problems is that these rules are developed by a group of experienced physicians sitting around a table and saying 'based on my experience, this is what should happen.'

"Even if you assume that they are properly taking into account the likelihood (probability) of a certain result, they still have to evaluate it against other results. They come up with a gut reaction that's their best guess on what most patients would want. When you have a model, what you're doing is using the actual outcomes and information based upon the statistics regarding what happens at this particular hospital or region of the country, whatever the database may be. So the model really relies on evidence-based medicine."[3]

There are other challenges associated with the old "gather the doctors around a table" approach to setting standards. "With paper based guidelines, you have to get the doctors to sit around the table again after they have had experience with a new procedure, and it takes a year or more for new procedures to work their way into practice guidelines," Raker observes. "You're not subject to these delays if you're working off of models. As soon as a new procedure comes out you can enter it into the model and the model will adapt."

Possibly more than any other industry today, healthcare is an extraordinarily complex and interdependent web of individual and organizational stakeholders. Each stakeholder has vital information – for example regarding the efficacy of treatments, costs, preferences, demographics, unique combinations of circumstances and medical conditions, etc. – that would be of benefit to at least some other stakeholders in the system. Each stakeholder would also benefit from the information provided by many others in the system. TreeAge Software's

DATA Interactive is a first step toward realizing the dream of an interactive knowledge management system that potentially could reach across the slowly dissolving boundaries among the stakeholders in the healthcare industry.

Advances in decision modeling and the ubiquity of the Internet bring this dream closer to reality than ever before. Even so, "the whole thing about the Web is that this is all very much in the development phase, particularly in the medical area" says Morris Raker. "If people start using DATA Interactive for clinical treatment, then surely it will move to the Web, whether intra- or inter-net. It ultimately ought to work like this: patient record systems are being updated all the time with patient information. When a patient is making a treatment decision, the physician will go into his or her computer terminal and specify certain information. Based upon that information the appropriate model will come up in the form of the questions that have to be answered about this particular patient. The desirability of different treatments will vary for each patient depending upon characteristics of the patient (e.g. smoker, prior surgery, cancer, etc.) You have the basic information in the model, but then you have the possibility of adapting the model for the particular patient. And some of that patient's information may be automatically filled in from the patient's information stored in the hospital or health-system's database.

"Based on that information, a recommended treatment decision may come up. Or it might be set up in such a way that the physician will type in the recommended treatment, the same way they might type in a prescription, and the computer will check their recommendation against the model. If the model comes up with treatment B and the doctor has recommended treatment A, the system will show why it recommends B. This decision should be made in consultation with the patient where the patient has full information about the consequences, and not simply determined by the patient's doctor, as it generally is today.

"That's the way it ought to ultimately work. The model you see is going to be tied into the hospital's computers, which may in turn be tied into national outcomes information for different types of treatments, effectiveness and cost information for the hospital, region, and state, etc., and this information will be constantly updated. As these systems are implemented, information on outcomes will automatically be entered into the system and become available."

Mike Aristedes is co-founder of M-Tag (Medical Technology Assessment Group, www.m-tag.net), a leading health technology assessment consultancy based in Australia and the UK. Mike specializes in economic evaluation of healthcare interventions. He quips "I'm in the coin flipping industry, but it takes a lot to get there . . . Economic evaluation is a major analytic technique for decision analysis. It's a method that lets you compare a number of interventions according to their respective costs and outcomes. It therefore enables the construction of cost effectiveness, or value-for-money information. Based on the information, the decision-makers must decide whether they are willing to spend money on that."[4]

As Morris Raker points out, "in any situation in which you have limited resources, how do you distribute that pie? Somewhere someone has to say that society isn't going to pay a million dollars to extend life by one year for someone. Any time you have limited resources you have to determine how you're going to allocate those funds, and that's done by cost-effectiveness in the medical field. It's going on all the time, but generally by the seat of one's pants so to speak. Our software is a way to do this based on evidence."

Mike Aristedes concurs: "We've now gotten to the point where economic evaluation is an important aspect of healthcare economics. Its biggest role is its use in pharmaceutical funding decisions – decisions to fund new pharmaceuticals. That is its biggest global use, pioneered in Australia in 1993. I contributed to this as part of a team responsible for implementing and administering the first formal policy requirements for economic evaluation in healthcare. It's basically a policy system so that when pharmaceutical companies want a pharmaceutical funded, they have to provide data in the form of an economic evaluation to support their case.

"This really is somewhat of a revolution in the pharmaceutical area for both the regulators as well as the industry. The health bureaucracies around the world are slowly introducing these requirements for economic evaluation in healthcare, and the major focus is on pharmaceuticals. These new requirements are not universal. For example, the US does not have universal requirements for economic evaluation, though some HMOs consider economic data in their decision making as to whether to fund a new drug. However, there are universal requirements in the UK, Canada, and Australia."

Given the potential market for new pharmaceuticals and the costs associated with developing them, the stakes are incredibly high. For example, "in Australia, probably about 20 economic evaluations are presented to the health department each quarter, which funds pharmaceuticals on a national basis," says Aristedes. "If you get approved by them then your drug is subsidized by the government, and probably about half of them are using decision analysis to help them generate their data for economic evaluation. So the stakes are very high. Decision analysis is used so frequently so that the health department reviewers will look at these analyses, and make national decisions partially using the decision analysis information. It's a fascinating situation."

Yet even though decision analysis is being elevated to the level of government mandate, it does not obviate the need for some deep soul-searching in the face of high stakes decisions. Mike Aristedes reflects: "it is really interesting, but fundamentally I think that the decision-maker still has to make decisions, and all of this stuff is an aid, but it does not replace what's called the sovereignty of the decision-maker. I've been on these decision-making committees in the pharmaceutical area and I've seen decision-makers agonize over decisions, even with the support of the data and the models."

Thus rational decision-making processes are playing an increasingly pivotal role in the healthcare industry. While this may be a vast improvement over prior, "seat of the pants" evaluative techniques, it remains a necessary but insufficient condition for effective decision making. Rapid, easy access to high quality information and analytic models and tools is essential, but it still may leave the decision-maker at the threshold of an incredibly difficult moral precipice.

COMPLEMENTING RATIONALITY WITH INTUITION

Intuition plays a key role in effective decision making. Yet there has been very little applied research on the use of intuition in management decision making.[5] It should also come as no surprise that you won't find intuition on a business school syllabus. Of course, intuition and other soft decision-making skills are difficult, some would say impossible, to teach. As a result, business schools tend to ignore the fact that these soft decision-making skills are a vital element of effective decision making. Unfortunately, without these skills, all that managers have to guide them is the cold, hard hand of logic, with its backward looking analysis and limitations.

To make matters more challenging, we don't really know what intuition is or exactly how it works. Fortunately, we have some clues. When managers are asked what they think intuition is they offer a wide variety of answers. Research carried out by Dr Jagdish Parikh at IMD, the famous business school based in Lausanne in Switzerland, for example, involved asking 1300 senior managers from nine different countries what they thought intuition was.[6] Their most frequent answers were: (1) decision/perception without recourse to logical/rational methods (23.4%); (2) inherent perception, inexplicable comprehension, a feeling that comes from within (17.1%); and (3) integration of previous experience, processing of accumulated information (16.8%).

Parikh's research also drew comparisons between countries. He found that Japanese managers said they used intuition most frequently in their work, a finding supported by other research into Japanese management. American managers ranked second highest, and the British came in third.

More recently, researchers Naresh Khatri and H. Alvin Ng studied the role of intuition in strategic decision making. They propose the following definition based on their synthesis of the prior research on intuition: "Intuition is not an irrational process. It is based on a deep understanding of the situation. It is a complex phenomenon that draws from the store of knowledge in our subconscious and is rooted in past experience. It is quick, but not necessarily biased as presumed in previous research on rational decision making."[7]

Khatri and Ng surveyed 281 executives from 221 companies in the banking, computer, and utility industries in the northeastern US. Those three industries were purposefully chosen to represent varying degrees of environmental turbulence. The researchers focused on three aspects of intuition: judgment, past experience, and "gut-feeling," which taken together comprise what they call "intuitive synthesis." Interestingly, their findings suggest that:

» managers frequently rely upon intuitive synthesis, especially its experience and judgment aspects, when making strategic decisions;

» computer industry executives use "gut-feel" to a much greater extent than do executives in the banking and utility industries;

» all three aspects of intuitive synthesis contribute significantly to financial performance; and

» intuition plays a more critical role when making strategic decisions in volatile environments, but should be used with greater caution in stable and somewhat unstable contexts.

Based on these findings, the researchers raise several important questions for future research: (1) is it possible to develop one's intuition and, if so, how? (2) is intuition derived from experience transferable to similar situations or contexts? and (3) does combining intuition and rational analysis yield better results than primary reliance on one or the other?

Given the continued escalation of turbulence in most business environments, the researchers suggest that intuition will become increasingly important in strategic decision making.

A SPIRITUAL COMPASS FOR DECISION MAKING

"Alright," you might be thinking, "hold on to your horses. Just as managers are finally beginning to warm up to the idea that 'soft skills' like intuition may play a vital role in effective decision making, and there's some rational data to support that, you try to take us over that Spiritual edge. Just how far out are we going here? After all, this still is about *business,* isn't it?"

Well, yes of course. But even the Academy of Management, the premiere professional association of management academics with 10,000 members in 80 countries, and publisher of two of the top tier management journals, now has a "Management, Spirituality, and Religion" (MSR) interest group (http://aom.pace.edu/msr). The purpose of the interest group is to "encourage professional scholarship in the relationship between management, spirituality and religion." It has more than 1000 members, and courses are being developed in an increasing number of universities to explore these topics. And none other than *Fortune* magazine featured "God & Business" as its cover story on

July 9, 2001. The story revealed the extent of this largely grassroots movement in the US. Spirituality is definitely happening in business.

Management Professor Andre L. Delbecq heads the Institute for Spirituality of Organizational Leadership at Santa Clara University in Santa Clara, CA. He is a highly regarded member of the Academy and an active member of the MSR interest group. He told *Fortune*, "There were two things I thought I'd never see in my life . . . the fall of the Russian empire and God being spoken about at a business school".[8]

But just how does this relate to managerial decision making? Delbecq has been co-ordinating an ongoing dialogue among theologians, senior executive, and management scholars on the ways in which religious traditions provide insight into management. "One of the places is in decision making," he says, "so we've been looking at the rich tradition of discernment as the Christian term, but also at the way in which that's echoed in the writings of Taoism, Buddhism, Judaism, Islam, and the Hindu tradition."

"The Center itself and my work in this area are inspired by senior executives who asked for a course that deals with that deep inner life of the leader, because to be a senior leader is really to stand at the edge of unknowing. You are leading people toward a future that doesn't exist, with all of its uncertainties, and unless you can enter into that with some sort of inner compass you can't sustain your courage when you begin to encounter the difficulties, setbacks, confusion, and angst of that path. So there really was a demand for this.

"I think there was a time when we held jobs and did work and lived much of our lives outside of work. But for the present knowledge worker and especially the leader, what's being asked of you is your entire self, your mind, your spirit, your creativity, your energy. And if you're going to give all of that then you're going to want it to have a deep spiritual meaning because it really is going to be the center of your life, and people want to devote their lives to something that matters. I think the majority of leaders see the spiritual, and want to touch that deep self in the process of their leadership."

Discernment, according to Delbecq, involves "experiencing, understanding, and committing to the presence and guidance of God in our decisions" and "seeking the freedom to make choices which lead to the fullness of our human potential and to greater participation in God's life." But what if you are not a religious person? "For most people there is a sense of the transcendent," Andre says. He notes that some have defined spirituality as "a worldview plus a path, so even if you have a non-religious worldview and a very secular path, it is that very deep integrating inner path that spirituality touches."

You might be wondering how this relates to intuition, if at all. Andre explains the distinction. "In the Christian tradition it's the belief that if you can rest in listening, you can discover the will of God," he says. "If you can remain centered and rest in God and listen, you can discover God's will. Sometimes God's will is quite surprising and contrary to what you want. So those people who believe in God believe that it goes beyond one's intuition, because sometimes what we call our intuition is simply our fear, anxiety, or our dark side speaking to us. Hence discernment gets to the deep inner self below the level of ego in relationship with the transcendent."

Delbecq believes that rationally based decision processes and discernment are highly complementary. He cites three primary reasons for failed strategic decisions that discernment can overcome: undue reliance on self and on science, and under-involvement of others. He suggests an integrated discernment/decision process involving six steps.

1 Enter with a reflective inner disposition (ignored in rational processes).
2 Have patience in discovering underlying decision issues. In the discernment tradition this involves "watchful waiting," indecision, and detachment from distortions, whereas in the decision process tradition it involves listening to multiple stakeholders and scouting for external ideas.
3 Gather information – a forte of the rational approach, not well utilized in discernment.
4 Reflection and prayer, which involves being centered, reflecting on sacred writings, inner attention, and remaining detached. The decision-making tradition has expanded to include emotion and intuition here, but remains biased toward speed and rationality.
5 Tentative decisions, with attention to outcomes, which in discernment involves "holistic confirmation," not simply the "bottom line."
6 Future re-evaluation, which is an integral feature of both traditions.

"Holistic confirmation" may in fact aid in the process of effective implementation by sensing the early warning signs of trouble which standard metrics may miss entirely. For example, "it's very easy to take certain instrumental cues, like numbers added or extent of market penetration and have short run success even though people see other things that are dysfunctional and creating ill ease," Andre explains. "Those successes become reified into 'whole truth,' while at the same time people are actually feeling a little uneasy about them, or they are not sure they are going to be able to meet the deadline, etc. If you pay attention to people's spirit and make them comfortable in being able to communicate their areas of concern you'll pick up nuances that you're going to miss simply from the instrumental indicators. I have a friend who is a CEO of a major contract construction firm who says that paying attention to [these] messages alerts you to unanticipated outcomes and unintentional early warning of dysfunctional outcomes."

Delbecq also believes that "DSS plays a very critical role. It's one of the contributions of contemporary social science and decision-science. We now have tools that allow us to access knowledge and information; that's a very powerful aid to any discernment process. The end of the discernment journey is the discovery of truth; so all of the techniques that help you to discover what is true are helpful. The difficulty of course is the way that science parses its investigation is that you know more and more about less and less. You can be overwhelmed with specificity, so the discernment tradition keeps you focused on what are the themes that you should be looking for as you sort through that information? What are the values that you need to be anchored in as you look at all of that data? What are the voices that you should listen to that might otherwise be excluded? So it really gives you a way of being centered and calibrated in the midst of the explosion of information.

"I think it's very easy to turn speed into a false idol and to use it as an excuse to shortcut information gathering, to exclude certain voices, to move precipitously on a single preference, etc. So it is true that things move more rapidly simply because the totality of the system is more interconnected, but I think you can also move precipitously and carelessly, so finding that balance is aided greatly by the process of discernment." (You may recall that undue speed, truncated information gathering, and under-involvement of others were all implicated in the high failure rates of executive decisions,[9] as discussed in Chapter 1.)

For those who may be interested in developing a contemplative practice, whether to support their decision making or simply to live richer lives, "the first step is always to deepen the spiritual journey in whatever one's tradition may be," Andre says, "so if you're a Buddhist, it's to deepen one's practice in that tradition, in Christianity it's the movement into a contemplative dimension of one's tradition, because the entry point in discernment is always out of that contemplative meditative presence. It's very ancient. There is an enormous resurgence of interest in contemplative practice in our present time, both East and West."

It is also possible to develop organizational support for the integration of discernment into decision-making processes. Examples may be found in some surprising places. "For example," according to Andre, "in the old tradition the abbot is obligated to make decisions that affect the entire monastery, must engage in consultation with all of the monks, is enjoined to listen to the young monks first so that their freshness of insight is heard before they are intimidated by what some of the older monks might say. So from the very earliest monastic times to the present, we have norms regarding participation, admonitions to listen to people who are new and fresh to the organization, the need to consult with all of the stakeholder voices, the movement to negotiation and win-win solutions as opposed to forcing or smoothing, so there are ways in which normative structures can be introduced to the group that are compatible with the rules of discernment."

Looking ahead, Delbecq describes some of the possibilities and challenges of integrating spirituality into our workplaces, and thereby into our decision making. He says, "I think there's been a sort of personal as well as national schizophrenia in terms of deeply held values that we apply to our family life and even to our patriotic national life and to business. It's been as if the Saturday/Sunday chasm doesn't enter into Monday through Friday. And it's as if people had to check their deep spiritual path at the door on Monday and pick it up again on Friday, or at the end of the workday. What we are seeing is that people don't want to live their lives that way. Finally they can begin to bring complete self, and the richness of complete self, into the workplace. And when that happens, why we'll transform our workplace settings into more humane, more just, and more effective institutions. It's a complex moment in history because we know the dangers of interreligious conflict, and on the other hand we're beginning to understand that one can bring the richness of one's religious tradition and talk about one's spirituality without inappropriate proselytization in a way that's appreciative rather than conflictive and harmful.''

Certainly given history this is delicate territory. Yet Andre Delbecq is not alone. Thousands of other people believe that we have reached a point in social development in which diverse spiritual traditions may exist together in harmony and enrich life in the workplace of the twenty-first century and beyond. Whether organizations openly embrace these practices or not, thousands of executives are quietly integrating their spirituality into their decision-making processes.

A GLOBAL COMPASS FOR MANAGERIAL DECISION MAKING

Intuition and spirituality provide internal guidance and support for the individual manager in state-of-the-art decision processes. In the waning years of the twentieth century, templates for global decision making began to emerge in a variety of areas. These templates are designed to create a world system that works for everyone. For example, the ISO movement established (and continues to establish) standards for both product and service oriented organizations to achieve levels of quality that are recognized and respected throughout the world. State-of-the-art managerial decision making increasingly looks beyond organizational boundaries to integrate such global concerns into its deliberations.

Some of these global templates embody the highest hopes and possibilities for humanity. The Natural Step is such an exemplar. In the eighties, Swedish oncologist Dr Karl-Henrik Robert became obsessed with the search for solutions to the accelerating pace of environmental degradation. He catalyzed a collaborative interdisciplinary research effort into environmental sustainability involving 50 Swedish scientists in an extensive iterative process. The end result became the basis for a global template for environmental sustainability called The Natural Step. The program received support from the King of Sweden, then business and political leaders. Twenty independent professional networks (e.g.

doctors, farmers) were formed to disseminate and build consensus around the Natural Step (TNS) principles.

The purpose of TNS is to develop and share a common framework comprised of easily understood, scientifically-based principles that can serve as a compass to guide society toward a just and sustainable future. Since its inception in 1989, it is being used in numerous countries and more than 70 corporations, including Home Depot, Nike, Mitsubishi Electric USA, Collins Pine, the world's largest manufacturers of appliances (Electrolux), furniture (IKEA) and floor coverings (Interface), and Sweden's three major supermarket chains, biggest oil company, largest hotel chain (Scandic Hotels, one of the three success stories included in Chapter 7), and McDonald's. In addition, more than 70 municipalities, including both rural towns and urban cities like Stockholm, as well as public institutions such as the University of Texas at Houston Health Science Center, are working with The Natural Step guidelines.

At the core of TNS are four "system conditions," based upon laws of thermodynamics and natural cycles, which in essence may be expressed as, in order for a society to be sustainable:

1 the ecosphere must not be subject to increasing rates of substances that are extracted from the earth's crust (e.g. metals, petroleum);
2 it must also not be subject to increasing concentrations of substances produced by society (e.g. synthetic organic compounds like DDT, PCBs, and Freon);
3 natural systems also must not be systematically impoverished by physical displacement, over-harvesting, or other forms of ecosystem manipulation; and
4 resources must be used fairly and efficiently to meet basic human needs globally.

Dr Brian Nattrass and Mary Altomare are leading experts on the TNS framework, and the practice leaders on TNS for North America. They are co-authors of *The Natural Step for Business*[10] and *Dancing With the Tiger: Learning Sustainability Step by Natural Step.*[11] With operations in the US, Canada, and the UK (www.naturalstep.ca or www.naturalstep.org), Nattrass and Altomare consult for governments, municipalities, and Fortune 500 companies.

Mary explains what drew them to TNS. She says "I think part of what attracted us to this approach is that it didn't make business wrong. It recognized everyone's part in this. It's not a matter of saying who's to blame, but that we are all responsible. However, the business sector is the sector with the resources and levers to have a greater influence in determining whether the direction that the world is going in is more or less sustainable. We are all in it – there is no such thing as a sustainable organization in an unsustainable global society. The Natural Step Framework is scalable – you can apply it to yourself as an individual, your household, your business, your community, or nationwide. It's based on clear, basic science – that's another very clear strength to us. And it's science that most people have been exposed to in their learning if they have at least an eighth grade education.

"The other thing that we value about the approach of the Natural Step is that it doesn't say that the changes will happen overnight. We realize that a company not only has to stay in business but also to prosper. There are other benefits that come out of prospering, so in using this as a decision tool, you use it as a design criteria for your products and/or processes, for where you site your operations, and even how you build those sites. Nike, for example, has just built a world-class ecological European headquarters, so you can apply it to everything. How do your employees operate? How many have to commute to work? If you're a municipality, how does it apply to land use? To landfills? How do you maintain a golf course or street lighting? etc.

"Our experience with the companies and communities that we've worked with is that people generally want to do the right thing, but in order to do the right thing you have to be able to understand basic things about how the world works as an environmental system. What are the decisions that I can make that are in alignment with the laws of thermodynamics, for example that nothing disappears, that we can't truly throw things "away." Things don't disappear; they are building up in the global system. The way we change that is by each of us taking responsibility for decisions that we make, and by holding the companies and municipalities and governments that we work in, buy from, and live in, responsible.

"More and more people who are becoming aware that something needs to be done. There are some very prominent large corporations that are paying attention to this thing called sustainable development. We ourselves are working with Nike, Starbucks, The Home Depot, and CM2H Hill, a large engineering firm, IKEA, McDonald's in Sweden – these are companies that are really working on how do you integrate this thinking into the way we do business. There are no easy answers, and in my opinion, on a societal level this is something we are just figuring out together, and as we do this, companies need to stay strong in business. There are some very strong well-known companies that are saying YES this is our responsibility, and these companies will become examples and push it through their supply chains. A company that realizes that it is a system within systems within systems begins to look at the levers within the systems that it can push, and for many big companies it is the supply chain.

"The NS framework is simple enough, elegant enough, easily understood and based on science, that it has been a very attractive idea. One of the strengths of the Natural Step Framework is that it helps companies to understand whether any of these tools are actually helping it to move in a more sustainable direction or not. If you are looking at this as a decision support system, you might begin by saying does this lead us in a more sustainable direction, is there something we could design into our product that would eliminate a damaging impact from the very beginning. So you might actually design the product differently from the beginning.

"I think that there is a lot of attention being paid to it, and I think the direction of change is the right direction, but I don't know whether we are changing things quickly enough. We don't know what we're doing – we have this experiment that we are playing with, this global system that we are playing with, and we don't know what the outcomes will be and we don't have another planet to go to."

BEYOND PROBLEM-SOLVING

It's not likely that you will have noticed in the entire discussion of managerial decision making so far, that decision making is almost invariably associated with identifying and solving problems. If you did notice, you may not have thought anything of it. It makes sense to us as a basic, underlying assumption regarding managerial decision making.

Of course decisions are all about identifying and solving problems. After all, that's what managers are supposed to do, isn't it?

Well, perhaps. But there is a new movement which recognizes that the problem-solving assumption is a by-product of the lingering worldview of the universe as a machine – rooted in Newtonian physics as discussed in Chapter 3. If organizations are machines, they are naturally viewed as "problems to be solved." Find the parts that aren't working properly, tinker with them until they do, and if they can't be made to work, replace them. Thus until very recently, thinking and practice regarding management and managerial decision making were rooted in this problem-solving orientation. But we were largely unaware of it, and its limitations, just as fish are (as far as we know) oblivious to the nature of the water in which they swim.

There are new views of organizations, new models and metaphors, that transcend problem-solving approaches to management and decision making. One particularly effective and constructive approach is appreciative inquiry, which is based on the groundbreaking work by David Cooperrider in his 1987 dissertation at Case Western Reserve University,[12] and countless others in the growing global community of appreciative organizational practitioners. As David explains it "appreciative inquiry is about the co-evolutionary search for the best in people, their organizations, and the relevant world around them. In its broadest focus, it involves systematic discovery of what gives 'life' to a living system when it is most alive, most effective, and most constructively capable . . . Ai involves, in a central way, the art and practice of asking questions that strengthen a system's capacity to apprehend, anticipate, and heighten positive potential. It centrally involves the mobilization of inquiry through the crafting of the 'unconditional positive question' . . . Ai deliberately, in everything it does, seeks to work from accounts of this 'positive change core' – and it assumes that every living system has many untapped and rich and inspiring accounts of the positive."[13] (p. 3)

This is a marked departure from traditional problem-solving approaches, which may account for its increasingly well-documented effectiveness in organizations and communities of all sizes around the world. Paul Nutt[14] found that problem-solving was commonly used by managers, but not terribly effective. He explains that 'problem-solving tactics fail because the search for solutions is narrowed and defensiveness is evoked ... Listing problems makes people defensive because they see themselves as potentially accountable. This prompts them to maneuver to avoid becoming scapegoats and draws energy from the decision effort'. Thus problem-solving can result in tactics of blame and evasion.

Appreciative inquiry (Ai) also embodies another success factor identified by Nutt,[15] which is to include as many stakeholders who will be impacted by the decision in the decision process as possible. In its fullest expression, Ai is a "whole system" change process that invites the participation of everyone involved in an organization or community.

Perhaps the most powerful aspect of Ai is its choiceful focus on the nature of the questions that are asked. If we begin by trying to discover "what's wrong around here," it's no doubt that a host of problems and issues will be identified. If we seek to discover what's right, what's working, what inspires us, and to learn from that, then we will elicit stories of proud achievements and success. The mechanistic, problem-solving orientation assumes that elimination of problems equals desired performance. Does it? Might we not learn a great deal more by learning what contributes to outstanding productivity and effectiveness?

For example, typically in a customer service organization managers might look at the percentage of unsatisfied customers, try to find out why they aren't satisfied, elicit the underlying problems involved, and then solve those problems to reduce the number of complaints and dissatisfied customers. Certainly a valid, and common, approach. However, it may well prompt evasive tactics and blaming among the customer service personnel.

What if instead the manager were to engage in an appreciative inquiry involving all customer service personnel and customers to learn about times when customers were absolutely thrilled with the products or services that they received, and what made those experiences possible. People love to talk about their finest moments, about work that they are truly proud of. Then implement the factors that were present during outstanding service *across the board* – so that exceptional satisfaction becomes the norm. Amplify and build upon success! Design structures to support that. In the process it's likely that you will eliminate a lot of the problems that you *would* have identified in a problem-oriented approach, but as a wonderful by-product of a fully energized and engaging process.

Appreciative inquiry has profound implications for managerial decision making. What if we were to design appreciative system-wide DSS? Rather than criticizing corporations for environmental non-compliance, what if we were to learn what they are doing right, and amplify and collaboratively build on that, as The Natural Step is doing? What if we were to combine all of this with a deeply contemplative Spiritual appreciation for the gift that our planet and its precious resources are, including *all* people and living beings? These are some of the exciting and rapidly emerging possibilities for state-of-the-art managerial decision making in the twenty-first century.

KEY LEARNING POINTS

State-of-the-art decision making includes:

» rationality;
» rapid, easy access to relevant, high quality data;
» intuition;
» inner tranquility;
» global concerns;
» inclusion of all stakeholders; and
» appreciation, not just problem-solving.

NOTES

1 Author interview.
2 TreeAge provides state-of-the-art tools for decision analysis, cost-effectiveness analysis, Markov modeling, and Monte Carlo simulation in clinical decision making, epidemiological modeling, and pharmaceutical outcomes research.
3 Note: The Institute of Health Sciences at the University of Oxford (www.ihs.ox.ac.uk) is a key centre for evidence-based medicine.
4 Author interview.

5 Khatri, N. and Ng, A.H. (2000) "The role of intuition in strategic decision-making." *Human Relations*, January 2000.

6 Parikh, J. (1994) *Intuition: The New Frontier of Management*. Blackwell, Oxford, UK.

7 Khatri, N. and Ng, A.H., *ibid.*, p. 62.

8 Gunther, M. (2001) "God & business." *Fortune*, New York, 9 July.

9 Nutt, P. (1999) "Surprising but true: Half the decisions in organizations fail." *Academy of Management Executive* **13**(4).

10 Nattrass, B. and Altomare, M. (1999) *The Natural Step for Business: Wealth, Ecology and The Evolutionary Corporation*. New Society Publishers, British Columbia, Canada.

11 Nattrass, B. and Altomare, M. (2002) *Dancing With the Tiger: Learning Sustainability Step by Natural Step*. New Society Publishers British Columbia, Canada.

12 Cooperrider, D. "Appreciative inquiry: Towards a methodology for understanding and enhancing organizational innovation." *Dissertation Abstracts International*, University Microfilms No. 8611485.

13 Cooperrider, D. "Capturing what matters most in the practice of appreciative inquiry: A positive revolution in change." In: P. Sorensen (Chair), *Appreciative inquiry: Capturing what matters most - a review and assessment*. Symposium conducted at the annual meeting of the Academy of Management, San Diego, California, August, 1998.

14 Nutt, P., *ibid*.

15 Nutt, P., *ibid*.

In Practice: Success Stories

Making business decisions is as much art and craft as it is science. Three exemplary cases are presented that illustrate the nuances of the art, craft, and science of business decision making. The first case contrasts the strategies of Coke and Pepsi on entering the vast Chinese market. The second highlights factors that contributed to the successful implementation of DSS in the top specialty retailer of consumer electronics, personal computers, entertainment software and appliances in the US. The third tells the inspiring story of Scandic Hotels' integration of global environmental and social concerns into managerial decision making throughout the organization, and its stellar performance as a result.

» Successful strategic decision making: Coke vs Pepsi in China
» Best Buy: award winning success with DSS
» Values-centered decision support: Scandic Hotels

Theories and tools for successful decision making abound (refer to Chapter 9 for detailed examples), yet somehow the value and relative success of any particular decision may only be known through the eyes of history and the context within which the decision was made.

Great decisions are usually only realized in retrospect. Today's success story is yesterday's risky decision – and uncertainty is inherent in all risk. The outcome of any decision is unknowable in advance. Use of decision theories, tools, and support systems may help to reduce that uncertainty, but they cannot eliminate it, no matter how sophisticated those tools or theories may be.

Thus decision-making success "stories" are exactly that – retrospective tales of decisions that turned out well. They benefit from the perfect hindsight that historical perspective makes possible. Yet historical perspective is not fixed or absolute. It depends upon the cultural and temporal lenses used to view a particular success story. A decision may be considered "successful" when considered within a particular timeframe and organization, industry, and national context. Yet that same successful decision may undermine the broader strategic objectives or long-range viability of an organization. Winning a significant market battle – no matter how brilliantly – does not equal winning the war.

SUCCESSFUL STRATEGIC DECISION MAKING: COKE VS PEPSI IN CHINA

Coke and Pepsi, the "Hatfields and McCoys" of the corporate world, continue to engage in a global battle for soft-drink market dominance. Pepsi plays David to Coke's Goliath, valiantly, stubbornly, and cleverly trying to upset Coke's fortress of market leadership. Pepsi proclaims, "Never Say Never," while Coke turns a deaf ear, chanting: "Never say 'Pepsi'." Battles come and go; skirmishes are lost and won. The headlines trumpet decades of combat history: "Cola's thirst for battle,"[1] "How Coke is kicking Pepsi's can,"[2] "Pepsi takes on the champ,"[3] "Coke fights back,"[4] "Pepsi opens a second front,"[5] and "Guess who's winning the cola wars."[6]

Through the long history of this notorious intra-industry "war," legions of strategic decisions have come and gone as Coke and Pepsi fought to create and/or seize global soft-drink markets. The relative "success" of any significant decision made by these giants can only be gauged against the backdrop of their competitive strategic dance over time.

Comparing PepsiCo, Inc. to Coca-Cola may be unbalanced at best given the fact that Pepsi continues to compete in several different industries, including the non-carbonated drinks business (e.g. Aquafina water) which is growing faster than soft drinks overall, and Pepsi's complementary snack food business via industry giant Frito-Lay. Yet Pepsi earned its stripes in the trenches of the Cola Wars (see Table 7.1[7]), and revisiting those muddy trenches yields rich insights in contrasting Coke and Pepsi's strategic decisions regarding their forays into China.

Weighing in the two contenders

Company strategies both shape and are shaped by the decisions that their leaders make. Coke and Pepsi each made significant strategic decisions over time that either resulted in the development of new competitive competencies, or leveraged existing ones to their relative advantage. Here's a brief overview of some of the key decisions in their fight for the world soft-drink title.

In this corner: Coca-Cola's knockout strategic decisions

» *Knockout Decision #1*: Be First. Being first to market is generally a powerful source of competitive advantage, and Coke virtually invented the soft-drink industry. By 1902 it was the best-known product in the US, before Pepsi was even a gleam in its parents' eyes. Coke was also first into Western Europe, and it has frequently been first into other international markets, including China.

» *Knockout Decision #2*: Be Biggest – AND Be Flexible. Coke's sheer size and copious cash flow have served it well over time. They have given Coke the wherewithal to build a massive global soft-drink infrastructure, as well as to overpower most of Pepsi's potent marketing attacks. Yet Coke reaps the benefits of size and circumvents most of the downsides typically associated with size by being a virtual organization. Although Coke is formally "only" a concentrate producer, the "real" Coke packs a much larger punch. Coke competes internationally as a powerful alliance of soft-drink value chain organizations, including suppliers, bottlers, and distributors,

Table 7.1 The Cola Wars – a very brief history.

Coca-Cola	vs	Pepsi-Cola
Coke introduced.	1866	
Best known product in the US.	1902	
10:1 lead over Pepsi.	1940s	Almost bankrupt.
Government-assisted Cokes for 11 million troops in Europe in WWII.		
New brands, new countries.	1950s	One brand, one country (US).
Ignore competitors: "Never say 'Pepsi'".	1960s	Youth niche: "Pepsi Generation".
		Acquisition binge – including giant Frito-Lay.
Market leader: "It's The Real Thing" – best strategy for market leader.	1970s	Acquired Pizza Hut & Taco Bell to become 4th largest fast food chain in US.
Coke first into China – 1979.		"Pepsi Challenge" campaign.
Operating in 135 countries.	1980s	Pepsi leads in US grocery store segment for first time in history.
April 1985 – Scrap formula, introduce "New Coke".		
July 1985, brings back original Coke as "Coke Classic".		Mistakes in international management, e.g. Philippines
		Buys Seven-Up, #3 US soft drink.
Singular focus: Soft-drink market leader. Gushing in profits.	1990s	Became world's largest restaurant owner and third largest corporate employer.
Late 90s – restructuring, management turmoil, significant drop in brand and share value.		In late nineties copied Coke's lead, spun off fast food restaurants and many bottlers.

all banded together around Coke's #1 global trademark umbrella. Thus in a sense, Coke is both large and small at the same time. For example, in 1995–96 it operated in 200 countries with just 33,000 employees worldwide.

» *Knockout Decision #3*: Pump up your global brand. In 1996 Coke's brand was worth a cool $42.8bn.[8] By 1999 that value had nearly doubled to $83.8bn[9] (according to data from Interbrand/Citibank). Even though its brand value slipped 13% to $72.5bn in 2000, Coke will likely remain the world's top brand for the foreseeable future. It was the best-known product in the US in 1902, and it is the world's most widely recognized brand today. Coke's pervasive world-wide brand recognition augments its strategic advantage due to size.

» *Knockout Decision #4*: Be the "Real Thing." Coke has a winning formula for its syrup that only a handful of its elite have been privy to since Coke's inception. With the exception of the ill-conceived but thankfully brief abandonment of Coke's original formula in 1985 and the disastrous introduction of "New Coke," one of the company's great strengths has been the consistency of the taste of its product, and the management of its all-American image, over many generations.

» *Knockout Decision #5*: Retain the rights to sell directly to soda fountains. Unlike Pepsi, Coke originally retained the right to sell its syrup directly to fountains (which includes restaurants), a substantial – and highly profitable – market segment.

» *Knockout Decision #6*: Invest heavily in developing and maintaining a global soft-drink infrastructure. Effective infrastructure (e.g., supply, bottling, and distribution networks) is key in the soft-drink industry, and Coke's is king internationally. Coke shaped the entire industry's environment through massive investment in infrastructure.

» *Knockout Decision #7*: Develop and leverage powerful partnerships. Effective partnering is a key attribute of virtual organizations, and Coke has a long history of superb partnering, which is even more crucial to success in international markets. It chooses partners that are deeply networked into the infrastructure and mechanisms of the target market. A vivid example of this follows below in the discussion of Coke vs Pepsi in China.

And in this corner: Pepsi's perpetual crusade to beat the champ

This case mirrors Pepsi's historical dilemma. Coke came first. Coke gets top billing. Coke's advantages are well established in readers' minds before Pepsi even gets an opening to throw its first punch. In addition, Coke has been featured in at least twice as many periodical articles as Pepsi.[12] Pepsi's invasion of Coke's powerfully entrenched global network has therefore required strong opposition strategies. When considering Pepsi's configuration as a diversified conglomerate and its strategic decisions over the years, it is crucial to recognize that they were largely shaped in response to Coke's massive shadow.

» *Counter-Punch Decision #1*: Co-opt environmental threats. Co-opting has been one of Pepsi's key strategies, and it has had a profound impact on its structure and decisions. Pepsi co-opted its uncertainties in at least three major areas. First, until very recently it co-opted the bottler segment of its value chain via ownership of the majority of its bottlers – which are a critical and highly vulnerable link in the relatively simple soft-drink value chain. Second, Pepsi co-opted the fountain segment of its soft-drink market via ownership of its restaurant chains. Third, Pepsi has co-opted the competition whenever possible. For example, it purchased Seven-Up in 1986, thereby eliminating its main, although at the time weak, contender for the soft-drink industry's number two slot. It enabled Pepsi to better focus its energy on battling the giant above, instead of also having to defend itself against the threat of "the Un-Cola."

» *Counter-Punch Decision #2*: Make marketing magic. Pepsi is the marketing champ in the Cola Wars. In one stunning example, its "Pepsi Challenge" taste test vs Coke campaign in the early eighties boosted it to a two-point lead over Coke in the US supermarket segment for the first time in history. Even better for Pepsi, it prompted Coke to chuck its winning formula and introduce "New Coke," perhaps the most astonishing strategic and marketing blunder of the last century.[13]

» *Counter-Punch Decision #3*: Diversify to counter environmental turbulence. Pepsi's soft drink, snack food, and restaurant businesses have offset one another's downturns over time. For example, "In 1992, when beverage earnings dropped 7% thanks to the private-label wars with such companies as Cott, snack foods marched ahead with an astounding 30% increase in earnings, driven by the introduction of Doritos nacho cheese tortilla chips, one of Frito-Lay's most successful products . . . "[14]

» *Counter-Punch Decision #4*: Out-innovate the competition. Pepsi clearly wins the innovation trophy hands down.[15,16] Given Coke's market leadership position and the constancy of its taste and image over many generations, it makes sense that Coke would not tend to be a product innovator. Pepsi's Slice created the soft drink category of sodas that contain real fruit juice. Pepsi was the first to introduce a 100% NutraSweet soft drink (1984),[17] and CEO Enrico ushered in the trend in celebrity ad campaigns by signing Michael Jackson. These are just a few examples of Pepsi's aggressive innovations.

» *Counter-Punch #5*: Practice the art of competitive jujitsu. Christopher Sinclair, former chief executive of PepsiCo Foods & Beverages International, coined the term in the early nineties. As an opposition strategy, Pepsi locates and aims swiftly, directly and decisively at Coke's weaknesses. Pepsi throws Coke off balance by upsetting the rules of the marketplace.[18]

Pepsi and Coke are two very different companies. Their decisions and structures have been shaped by their respective strategies that, in turn, have been powerfully influenced by Coke's dominant position in the industry.

The Cola contenders invade China

Coke and Pepsi's historic structural, strategic, and cultural differences play out quite clearly and predictably in their decisions regarding entering the China market. For example, based on its strategic decision-making history, one might expect that Coke would have been first into China, that it would focus on developing soft-drink infrastructure, that it would choose substantial, well established international partners, that it would establish majority control with minority ownership in those joint ventures, and that it would plan long term. Pepsi might be expected to launch into China with an enormous marketing blitz, to use native entertainment stars in its advertisements, and to pursue smaller, local partners that it could control via majority ownership. That is in fact precisely what occurred.

Cultural context

Both Pepsi and Coke faced significant challenges to establishing a presence in China in the early 1980s, including: (1) the experimental nature of China's planned/market economy mix; (2) entry to China's market primarily through joint venture structures; (3) poor infrastructure throughout much of China's interior; (4) government control of most major distribution channels rendered them inflexible; (5) a highly fragmented and rapidly changing retail structure; (6) inconsistent water quality impacted the taste of fountain products; (7) the Chinese believed cola drinks may cause birth defects; (8) Chinese consumers were highly health conscious and preferred lemon-lime and orange drinks, which were viewed as being healthier alternatives; and (9) the difficulty of creating an appealing modern Mandarin translation for Coca-Cola and Pepsi Cola.

Given these challenges, the wise choice of joint venture partners was critical to the success of any foreign entry into the Chinese market. Superb partnering is one of Coke's fortes, and Coke partnered extremely well in China. The three partners that it chose supported its long-term focus on infrastructure development and overcoming the challenges inherent in China's economic development. Coke's partners structuralized its access to all of the resources it needed (e.g. trading, shipping, mining, sugar plantations, media, property, direct links to government) in order to make Coke available throughout China.

Pepsi, on the other hand, established 11 joint ventures with 10 different local companies (as of 1994). Pepsi generally opted for a 60% majority share in equity joint venture partnerships.[19] Given the high level of complexity inherent in establishing successful operations in China, Pepsi's diversity of partners could only have heightened dramatically the level of complexity it had to deal with. Consistent with its emphasis on flashy marketing, Pepsi led its Board of Directors on a high level relationship building tour of China in 1986.

In keeping with its ubiquity strategy, Coke's initial plants in China were more geographically dispersed than Pepsi's. Both Coke and Pepsi had to negotiate with the government for regional bottling franchise rights, and Coke took the lead in geographic coverage. As of late 1999, Coke had 24 bottling plants in China, garnered a third of its $3.5bn soft-drink market, was one of China's largest consumer-products companies, and its most familiar foreign brand, whereas Pepsi held only about a sixth of the Chinese soft-drink market and half as many bottling plants as Coke[20].

Developing brand recognition is critical to both Coke and Pepsi. In addition, names are extremely important to the Chinese. Therefore, designing an appealing and beneficial translation is paramount to the image and success of both company and product. Consistent with its long-range focus, Coke did a magnificent job in translating Coca-Cola into Mandarin in a way that sounds like Coca Cola and roughly translates as "tasty/delicious" and "evoking happiness." Pepsi's Mandarin translation, doesn't sound nearly as similar to Pepsi-Cola's English pronunciation, and its meaning is more akin to "everything interesting/funny" or "everything evoking happiness."[21] Worse, Pepsi's original translation of Seven-Up sounded like it meant "death from drinking" when pronounced in the Shanghainese dialect.[9]

Conclusion

Pepsi, in pursuing its niche strategy from the beginning in China, seems to have set itself up to play number two in what may one day become the world's largest soft-drink market. Overall, note the degree to which Pepsi's strategies have been structured – and its decisions made – in counterpoint to Coke's dominant position. Within this context, Pepsi's choices make more sense. Coke's sources of competitive advantage as market leader give it access to strategic choices that may not be available to Pepsi. What may be missed in focusing on Coke's industry dominance, however, is just how successful Pepsi has been given the enormous power and historic advantages of its arch-rival. After all, who said there's anything wrong with being number two?[22] Thus far, no other soft-drink company has even come close.

In the seventies, Coke would never have dreamt that Pepsi would one day outsell it in US supermarkets. Coke has powerful partners, infrastructure, and other formidable defenses that have fortified its leadership position. However, as Pepsi might proclaim from deep within the trenches: "NEVER SAY NEVER."

KEY INSIGHTS

» *Culture matters*: Not just the internal culture of the organization, but also the current and historical cultures of the relevant industries, and the national cultures in which the strategic decisions are to be implemented. And perhaps more important than any particular decision is the overall trend or "climate" of decision making that flows from a company's leadership and culture over time. These patterns might be thought of as a company's "strategic decision-making culture."

» *Competitive context matters*: The import of any particular decision may only be appreciated within the broader context of its competitive environments. For example, Pepsi's decisions to partner with numerous bottlers in China – though perhaps successful on a case-by-case basis – were clearly less successful than Coke's brilliant choice of substantial, multi-faceted infrastructure and resource partners with direct ties to top-level government.

» *Leadership matters – somewhat*: Perhaps the most amazing insight in reviewing the history of the Cola Wars over decades is not the breathtaking strategic coups masterminded by any particular Coke or Pepsi CEO, which the media love to draw attention to, but the relative consistency of their approaches to battle over time. Leadership matters, and any leader can make good or bad decisions, but industry and market environments seem to act as trueing devices, quickly snuffing out attempts to stray too far afield.

» *Perspective matters*: Pepsi's decision to own its restaurants and bottlers led it to become the world's largest restaurant owner, with vast real estate assets, and the world's third largest corporate employer, with 480,000 employees in 1995–96, whereas Coke's lean virtual organization employed a mere 33,000 during the same period[23] yet had profits nearly double Pepsi's. So which contender made the most successful decisions? From labor's and real estate's perspective, clearly it was Pepsi. From shareholder's perspective, Coke won hands down during those years. And what about from the earth's perspective? If the Earth could speak, what would it say about the global ubiquity of Coke – or Pepsi's fast food empire – and the impact on the Earth of their infrastructure, transport, and packaging? You choose the perspective.

» *Timeframe matters*: The relative brilliance of a decision only becomes evident over time. How much time? It all depends on your perspective. For example, Coke's decision to spin-off all but its core business and to become singularly focused was hailed by the Cola War correspondents throughout much of the nineties. But more recently some have expressed concern that choice may leave Coke vulnerable as the cola market runs out of room to expand, and non-carbonated drinks surge in popularity making colas in general somewhat passé.[24,25] Thus timeframe is critically important when considering stories of decision-making success.

BEST BUY – AWARD-WINNING SUCCESS WITH DSS

Minneapolis-based Best Buy Co., Inc. is the top specialty retailer of consumer electronics, personal computers, entertainment software, and appliances in the US. It operates retail stores and commercial Websites under the names: Best Buy (BestBuy.com), Magnolia Hi-Fi (MagnoliaHiFi.com), Media Play (MediaPlay.com), On Cue (OnCue.com), Sam Goody (SamGoody.com), and Suncoast (Suncoast.com). The company reaches consumers through more than 1700 retail stores nationwide, in Puerto Rico, and in the US Virgin Islands.

In August, 2001, Best Buy (www.bestbuy.com) and MicroStrategy® Incorporated (www.microstrategy.com), a leading worldwide provider of business intelligence software, received the Data Warehousing Institute's (www.dw-institute.com) prestigious Best Practices in Data Warehousing Award in the Performance Management category. Best Buy won the award for its MicroStrategy-based Business and Vendor Performance Application, which provides Web-based query and reporting capabilities to more than 2500 corporate and retail managers, as well as external partners. "We are delighted to have been selected as a winner of TDWI's prestigious Best Practices in Data Warehousing Award in Performance Management category for the success of our exceptional business intelligence application," said Clark Becker, senior vice president and chief technology officer for Best Buy. "With our MicroStrategy-based Business and Vendor Performance Management application, we are able to meet our objectives of equipping both our internal and external users with consistent and accurate information via a single, Web-based interface, while reducing costs."

This was no small achievement given the fact that 40–60% of data warehouse implementations fail (see Chapter 4). What enabled Best Buy to succeed where so many others fail? "Ironically the success had nothing to do with the software," says Randall Mattran, IS leader for Best Buy (the whole Information Systems management team uses that same egalitarian title). Randy is responsible for datawarehouse capability management, and the project managers that build the datawarehouse report to him. He says "it was the people from both companies working together in a story of partnership over a number of years that made it successful. Yes, the software worked and the right application was built. That was all well and good, but the real key to the success was that the marketing group and other business groups within Best Buy used process teams to help integrate a new application into the user base."

"The hardest thing in building these applications is to define the requirements correctly," Randy explains. "Marketing has their own process team. They have people dedicated to help define requirements and to make sure they are correct for the IS development team. The process team is also there to help people adopt the new capability. So it's marketing people training, supporting, and representing marketing users. Marketing has done a fantastic job of that."

Randy offers another example. "Retail operations have this thing called Standard Operating Platform (SOP). It is a set of procedures integrated with the applications that we build for them," he elaborates. "Each store can see how they are doing compared with other stores in their region. It is very competitive. They want to become #1; they are compensated based on their ranking. It's a dog-eat-dog mentality that seems to make things work in a retail store environment. So the stakes are high for them. It is all bonus-based. The Score Card reports that they generate through BPM give them the numbers they need to figure out where they are."

"MicroStrategy consulting also did a great job," Randy adds. "Any software by itself has no value until it is implemented correctly. The

MicroStrategy consulting team that we had onsite was able to interpret Best Buy's business needs and put "software to silicon" – so to speak – very effectively. Not every vendor has that strong capability. One thing that differentiated MicroStrategy was the quality and commitment of their consulting team."

Best Buy's BPM was developed as an integral part of a solution to a challenging set of circumstances. "In the history of Best Buy, there was a pretty rocky period late in fiscal year 1997," Randy says. "The company was expanding rapidly, but profitability was in jeopardy. Best Buy actually reported a net loss. When competitors see that, it's like a wolf smelling blood. Best Buy stock was split adjusted at around $2 at that point. So Andersen Consulting was retained to look at how the supply chain was managed and where profitability could be extracted from the current business. At that time Best Buy implemented the "Process to Profit" initiative, and that was the original source of the design for the BPM (business process management) application. There had to be reliable metrics that allowed Best Buy to get back to profitability. These reliable metrics were instruments in the dashboard that provided the guidance to tune our supply chain, get our inventory into the right locations, eliminate out of stock conditions, etc. So the Process to Profits initiative addressed several key issues, and the BPM was born to measure the Process to Profits metrics. The net result of that is that Best Buy has turned into one of the best performing retail stocks of the late nineties, and has been reasonably resilient to market conditions."

BEST BUY'S HISTORY – IN BRIEF

» **1966**: Best Buy's founder, chairman and CEO, Richard M. Schulze, launched Sound of Music, an audio component systems retailer.
» **1983**: Expanded into video. Became Best Buy.
» **1987**: Listed on NY Stock Exchange.
» **1989**: Retail innovation: began placing all inventory on the sales floor with non-commissioned product specialists.
» **1995–1997**: Rocky period – rapid growth, net loss, stock split at $2/share. Andersen Consulting hired. Partnered with Micro-Strategy in late 1996.

- **1996–1997**: "Process to Profits" initiative – develop reliable metrics.
- **1998**: Implement BPM system based on process to profits metrics.
- **Late 1990s**: Best Buy one of best performing retail stocks of late 1990s.
- **2000**: Opening at 60 stores per year.
- **2001**: Launches new Website to become a "bricks and clicks" retailer. 400 "brick and mortar" retail stores in operation in 41 states.
- **2004**: Goal to have 550 stores open nationwide.

Best Buy's successful DSS implementation

Best Buy's merchandise buyers typically start their workdays with coffee, some conversation about the weekend, and some intense Web browsing. But they're not surfing Yahoo.com or the local paper's home page. Instead, they point-and-click their browsers right to the company's BPM application, a "business intelligence system" based on MicroStrategy software that has become an essential component of their daily work. "They can't do their jobs as effectively without it," said Scott Heise, Best Buy's project manager for data warehousing, of the company's legion of more than 200 merchandise buyers. "The BPM yields critical insight that helps our buyers stock store shelves with products that move, keeping our carry-over costs at a minimum and our customers' needs met."

One measure of the success of a data warehouse implementation is its level of usage. If managers ignore the system and continue to rely on alternative data sources, it undermines the value and even the utility of the system over time. Randy Mattran provides some usage data on Best Buy's BPM. For example, "yesterday (12 September, 2001), 1300 users generated 84,000 scorecard reports. That's roughly 2 million per month. So the system is really used. I'm not sure if there is any other retailer that is doing that kind of volume from a data warehouse. That's one measure of the success of the implementation."

The process teams play a vital, ongoing role in supporting usage. They look at "what kinds of reports are being run, and by whom,"

Randy says. "If there's a particularly low volume user, they try to find out why. They usually find out that they are getting the information from some other source, and then they try to find out if it's a training or convenience issue. If they find out they are not using the system correctly, they will try to diagnose the cause. If it's training, that's easy to fix. But sometimes it's rebellion. Sometimes they don't trust the numbers. If they don't, that's a bad thing for us. Then we need to go back and find out where they can get the information from, and reconcile which source of information is the right one. Unfortunately, some systems are more right than others. And of course the correctness of the system is in the perception of the particular user. It takes a lot of explaining, auditing, and reconciliation to help people understand that the data warehouse can be their primary source of information. The process teams also try to share productive ways to use the system with other folks who might be able to use it in the same way."

How it works

MicroStrategy's business intelligence platform software anchors the BPM application and gives Best Buy users an array of options for data analysis and exploration. With a few clicks through a custom graphical interface (developed with Lancet Software, a MicroStrategy partner), users can run predefined reports ("Score Cards"), create their own queries and download information into Excel spreadsheets for easy off-line analysis right from their desktops. By tapping a single source of regularly updated data, BPM ensures the accuracy and consistency of information to support users in making effective decisions. "With the BPM, an executive instantly knows how his business unit is performing, and buyers know how the market has responded to their merchandise decisions," said Nancy Nelson, manager of the BPM project at Best Buy. "Whenever identified trends indicate potential problems, users can drill down into the data to get more detailed information, including sales by region, city, or even individual store."

Every time a Best Buy customer makes a purchase at one of its 400 (and rapidly growing) retail stores across the country, detailed data is collected about the transaction. For example, the brand of product the customer bought, the vendor that Best Buy bought the product from, the price it paid for the product and the price the customer paid. Best Buy collects these and countless other product and transaction attributes in an Oracle data warehouse. Through its BPM application, Best Buy gives its merchandise buyers, marketing teams, and executives desktop access to the collected information. "BPM enables merchandising, marketing, and buyer groups to evaluate trends and a broad range of metrics," Heise says. "Our vision is that BPM will become the platform on which the entire business makes its decisions."

Prior to implementing its BPM system, Best Buy managers relied upon various paper reports that were manually generated from several disparate data sources. They had to sift through multiple reports to access and integrate the information they needed. It was an inefficient process, and it frequently left specific questions unanswered. Best Buy managers needed detailed insight into current, accurate product sales and other data in order to make the most effective merchandise buying decisions, among others.

With the BPM in place, insight into product sales at all stores helps Best Buy managers identify trends, forecast sales, and make effective business decisions. It leads to lower inventory costs, stronger marketing, consumer-friendly store layouts, and a better bottom line.

"The benefits of the MicroStrategy application are a shared pool of accurate information, and universal access to it," said Heise. "It is having an enterprise-wide impact, and we think we can continue to leverage new applications into the BPM's MicroStrategy infrastructure." Indeed, Best Buy hopes to eventually roll out parts of the BPM application to its merchandise vendors to enable them to work proactively with buyers to help ensure that store shelves always meet customer product demands. The external application could increase supply chain efficiency, says Heise, an improvement that would translate directly into greater profitability.

The company is also considering implementing MicroStrategy Narrowcast Server™, an application that enables the delivery of critical sales and inventory reports through Web, wireless or voice. "Today at Best Buy, the data warehouse is not a distant IT solution," says Heise. "MicroStrategy has helped make it part of our employees" daily lives, and we expect it to continue yielding the insight required to run our business effectively."

KEY LEARNING POINTS

» *Partner well*: Best Buy exemplifies this in their choice of Micro-Strategy and Andersen Consulting. All three firms excelled in their commitment to co-evolving effective solutions over time. It's the story of effective trans-organizational collaboration over a number of years. As Randy Mattran puts it, "Technical innovation, skilful implementation, and good project management are all great, but you can only get the kind of results that Best Buy has been able to achieve if you are able to develop synergy between business thinkers and technology innovators." The partnership enabled them to do just that.

» *Analyze carefully*: A significant investment in up-front and ongoing analysis and thinking is essential to designing, building, and implementing an effective DSS. Best Buy excelled at this.

» *Measure what matters*: If you analyze carefully before you barrel ahead with a DSS, you are more likely to discover what matters most to measure, and to develop and/or refine metrics that do just that. These custom metrics then become the basis for building and/or adapting your DSS.

» *Involve others*: Need more be said? Involve users from the beginning, and throughout the process, in a substantive way. Best Buy achieved this by implementing process teams that helped facilitate the effectiveness of the partnership.

VALUES-CENTERED DECISION SUPPORT: SCANDIC HOTELS

Scandic is the leading hotel company in the Nordic region, with 153 hotels in 10 countries, and approximately 7000 employees in 2000 with a turnover of SEK 9bn. But it wasn't always this way. President and CEO Roland Nilsson was brought on board during the dark days of 1992 when Scandic was rapidly sinking in an icy cold sea of accumulated losses amounting to SEK 350mn (about $50mn). Times had been changing, and Scandic had fallen out of step. Nilsson led the company in an extraordinary, award-winning, values-centered turnaround that has made it a beacon for the possibility of socially conscious business.

SCANDIC'S HISTORY – IN BRIEF

» **1963**: Exxon launches as Esso Motor Hotel chain in northern Europe.
» **1992**: Scandic struggling for survival. CEO Nilsson hired.
» **1993**: Nilsson met with the founder of The Natural Step, Dr Karl-Henrik Robert, and invited him to make a presentation to Scandic management. Managers called the presentation "life-changing." Decision to adopt The Natural Step.
» **1994**: Environmental plan and policy presented to senior management. Enthusiastic support for "becoming one of the most environmentally friendly hotel chains." Creation of "Environmental Dialogues" company-wide training program.
» **1995**: 1500 environmental operational suggestions generated by staff – and implemented!! "Eco-room" first introduced.
» **1996**: First dedicated hotelier listed on Stockholm Stock Exchange.
» **1998**: Sales up 35%; net income up 60%.
» **1999**: Earnings/share up 50%. Scandic's "eco-hotel" wins European Hotel Design and Development Award.
» **2001**: Leading hotelier in Nordic region; acquired by Hilton Group plc.

Scandic's environmental decision-support program

Scandic operationalized the Natural Step principles (see Chapter 6) into a set of environmental criteria that guide decision making throughout the organization. Those criteria include:

» successfully integrate the principle of recyclability throughout Scandic's operations;
» comply with established laws and norms regarding the environment, and be one step ahead whenever possible;
» develop products and services that utilize natural resources as gently as possible;
» choose renewable raw materials, materials, and packaging that do not hurt the environment. Replace or remove products that fall short of these goals whenever possible;

» strive to use environmentally safe and renewable energy sources, and to use technology and distribution systems that have the minimum possible environmental impact;
» reduce waste through safe and responsible methods;
» choose, influence, and train Scandic's suppliers to participate in the fulfillment of its environmental objectives; and
» evaluate environmental results annually, and conduct environmental audits to ensure ongoing progress.

From the very beginning, Scandic walked its talk. Through its "Environmental Dialogue" program, it provided training for all employees so that they would understand the underlying ecological principles. As a result, 8000 employees participated in the design of Scandic's environmental programs.

Scandic then established the infrastructure necessary to ensure that environmental principles are integrated into decision processes at all levels throughout the organization. Environmental managers were established at each hotel who are responsible to a national Environmental Coordinator in each operational region and to the corporate Environmental Department in Stockholm. In addition, Scandic implemented two measures to track the results of its environmental programs throughout the chain: (1) an "eco-index" that clearly indicates how much environmental progress the hotels have made, and (2) SUS (Scandic Utility System), which enables them to monitor changes in resource usage over time.

The fruits of Scandic Hotels environmental initiatives

In the seven years since the inception of its environmental programs based on the principles of The Natural Step, Scandic Hotels has implemented over 2000 environmental initiatives, both large and small. Highlights include:

» In 1995 Scandic designed and introduced "eco-rooms" in which fixtures and furnishings are chosen with the greatest possible consideration for the environment. For example, synthetic materials, plastics, and metals are replaced with Nordic wood and pure wool fabrics wherever possible, resulting in a room that consists of 97% recyclable material, and that minimizes materials removed from beneath the earth's crust. Scandic's long-term goal is make its eco-rooms 100% recyclable. More than 8000 eco-rooms have been created so far.

» Scandic has launched the next level of environmental design with eco-hotels, in which its environmental principles are considered in every aspect of hotel construction, including choice of materials, functional efficiency, and recyclability. In the process it's created the "Scandic Environmental Construction Standard," which will serve as a corporate guide for all remodeling and new construction.

» Through its "Resource Hunt" program, designed to promote the efficient use of resources, Scandic reduced its carbon dioxide emissions by more than 15% and energy costs by more than 20% between 1997 and 1999. It also achieved a greater than 13% reduction in water consumption per guest, and a whopping 40% reduction in the volume of unsorted (unrecycled) waste. Further, Scandic implemented stringent demands on its suppliers to minimize packaging.

» In 1996 Scandic introduced its trend-setting "Soap & Shampoo Program," which involved replacing millions of disposable packages with hygienic dispensers in order to minimize waste and emissions.

» Scandic implemented its "Cleaning is an Art" program to train housekeeping personnel in using the right cleaning product in the appropriate amount for every job so as to reduce unnecessary and inappropriate usage.

» In 1999 Scandic Hotels became the first hotel chain to introduce KRAV-labeled breakfasts. KRAV is a nationally recognized form of eco-label in Sweden. Labeled items on the breakfast buffet table include coffee, teas, milk, oats, crisp bread, muesli, cheese, and so on. Given that the hotel chain serves 3.5 million breakfasts in Sweden each year, this action creates a significant market for the products of environmentally sustainable agriculture, in addition to raising consumer awareness.

Scandic's innovations have not only enriched its environmental bottom-line, but also contributed to its financial success. Scandic believes that its environmental program contributes significantly to its competitiveness and long-term success. By caring for the environment and being committed to social development, Scandic sees itself as co-creating a long-term community of values with its customers and other stakeholders by meeting their increased demands for environmental stewardship. A few economic indicators are provided in Table 7.2.[26]

Table 7.2 Scandic Hotels – financial success.

Indicator	1998	1999	2000	1st Q 2001
Net income	SEK 274mn	SEK 372mn	SEK 460mn	SEK 84mn
% increase	60%	36%	24%	29%
Sales	SEK 5004mn	SEK 5320mn	SEK 5971mn	SEK 1622mn
% increase	35%	6%	14%	28%
Operating margin	6.2%	6.7%	7.6%	5.0%
Earnings/ Share	SEK 9.79	SEK 4.64	SEK 6.67	SEK 0.92
% increase	–	+50%	+44%	–
Hotels added	22	17	8	4
Increased room capacity	20%	10%	15%	–

On April 23, 2001, Hilton Group plc announced a public offer to Scandic's shareholders and warrant holders. That same day Scandic's board of directors unanimously recommended acceptance of the offer to its shareholders. They continue to operate as Scandic Hotels in Scandinavia.

This all may seem like an environmental fairy tale, perhaps a bit too good to be true. Mary Altomare Nattrass, a leading authority on implementing The Natural Step, puts the story into perspective. "Scandic Hotels went from being on the brink of disaster to being a really choice plum to be picked. It's a really great success story in terms of how The Natural Step can be successfully integrated. And they are hard-nosed business people in a very competitive industry that is very sensitive to economic downturns, upswings, etc."[27]

Awards received

Scandic's deep integration of the Natural Step principles throughout its strategic and operational decision-making processes has earned it recognition not only in the financial markets, but also in the public eye. The company has received numerous local and international awards, including:

» the Environmental Stand Award, sponsored by World Travel Market (one of the world's largest travel trade fairs), and the environmental organization, The Green Globe;
» the Greening of Business Tourism Award, from EIBTM, Europe's biggest travel and incentive trade fair, EIBTM, for "a focus on the environment which is both all-embracing and represents a new approach";
» Scandic Hotel Byporten in Oslo, on the vanguard of Scandic's new "eco-hotels," received the European Hotel Design & Development Award in 1999; and
» two Scandic hotels thus far have been given the Nordic Swan eco-label. The Swan is the official eco-label of the Nordic countries, under the supervision of the Nordic Council of Ministers. As an independent, non-profit, industry-neutral body, the Swan verifies that certified hotels meet stringent environmental standards, as well as high standards for human health, functionality, and quality. The award is highly regarded in Sweden, and 91% of Swedes know what it stands for.

Ragnar Unge, president of SIS Miljömärkning, which administers the Nordic Swan in Sweden, commented that "Scandic Hotels was very quick off the mark when it came to stressing environmental issues and its position in the hotel industry as a whole has consistently increased ever since, so their further work on Nordic Swan certification is of considerable symbolic importance. The approval of the Scandic Hotel Continental will further reinforce the demand for Nordic Swan-labeled hotels and this will allow us to boost the tempo of our environmental efforts, the key goal of which is a sustainable society."

In addition, CEO Nilsson was named "Leader of the Year" in Sweden by the recruiting company Futurestep and the Affärsvärlden business weekly. According to Arne Mårtensson, CEO of Handelsbanken and a member of the jury panel for the award, "decentralized service companies must be managed with values and corporate culture. This is why they are interesting from a viewpoint of leadership. Roland Nilsson

has done an outstanding job with this decentralized service company."
Indeed he has.

Omtanke: positive, caring attention

Building on the breathtaking success of its environmental initiatives,
Scandic Hotels rolled out a new program in 2001 called "Scandic in
Society." Scandic's broad new vision is to become "a good company
in a good society" by contributing to and enriching its people, its
stakeholders, and society. The heart of the program is "Omtanke,"
which means positive, caring attention.

Omtanke is Scandic's core value to help it develop in a sustainable
direction along a triple "bottom-line" that includes not only economic
value-added, but also environmental and social enrichment. Omtanke
forms basis for relationships with Scandic's staff, customers, shareholders, and society. Scandic has created an "Omtanke Compass" to
help guide it in realizing its vision of becoming a good company in
a good society. The compass is essentially a pie-chart diagram that
depicts seven key interactive aspects of its vision: society, employees,
security, environment, health, business ethics, and human respect. The
company strives to be a role model in each of those areas.

The expanded vision is being implemented in the footsteps of
the environmental dialogues. In the first quarter of 2001, all Scandic
employees in the Nordic countries engaged in half-day dialogues to
discuss and define what a good company stands for and how it should
act. Specially trained "Omtanke Coaches" led these dialogues at every
hotel. The dialogues are intended to kick-off a long-term, ongoing
process of engagement with social and ethical questions that will lead
to the development of local and chain-wide programs.

By all measures, Scandic Hotels is a tremendous success. Having
already far exceeded what most businesses would consider to be
environmentally responsible, the company is fully energized as it
boldly designs a new future and deepens its commitment to its newly
expanded core values. Imagine a proliferation of decision support
systems for business that serve as value-compasses in business ethics,
environmental and social enrichment, and employee and customer well
being, in addition to financial success. What a gloriously wonderful
world it will be.

KEY LEARNING POINTS

» *Sustainability pays.* It's no longer a question of either/or, but both/and. Scandic's exemplary commitment to its environmental initiatives strongly supports its financial success. Scandic's continuing success in integrating TNS principles throughout its systems also provides a solid base from which to broaden its program to address additional facets of the role of "Scandic in Society."

» *No Lone Rangers.* The days of the Lone Ranger are over. Global concerns cannot be addressed by any single organization working in isolation. As Mary Altomare notes, "there is no such thing as a sustainable organization in an unsustainable global society" (Chapter 6). Your organization is either contributing to sustainability, or not. Choose, while you still can.

» *Ignite passion.* Roland Nilsson tapped into the deep concerns of Scandic's personnel and customers. He inspired them with a powerful new values-based vision for Scandic, and involved them in its ongoing creation and implementation.

» *Operationalize your values, and use a good compass.* Once you are clear about your values, operationalize them. Integrate them into every facet of planning and operations. And guide decision-making throughout your organization by using a well-developed compass. As your organization increasingly walks its values-based talk, it will inspire your workers, your customers, and the rest of the world.

NOTES

1 Reis, A. (1985) "Colas' thirst for battle." *Marketing*, 36–37, 21 November.

2 Sellers, P. (1996) "How Coke is kicking Pepsi's can." *Fortune*, 70–84, 28 October.

3 (1978) "Pepsi takes on the champ." *Business Week*, 88–97, 12 June.

4 Goff, N. (1980) "Coke fights back." *Financial World*, 17–20, 15 September.

5 Sellers, P. (1994) "Pepsi opens a second front." *Fortune*, 70–76, 8 August.

6 McLean, B. (2001) "Guess who's winning the Cola wars." *Fortune*, 2 April.

7 Information compiled from the other references cited for this case.

8 Sparks, D. (1996) "Will Pepsi take the Wall Street challenge?" *Financial World*, 26–29, 8 April.

9 http://www.marketing.haynet.com/

10 Seet, R. and Yoffie, D. (1995) "Internationalizing the cola wars (a): The battle for China and Asian markets." *Harvard Business School Case #9-795-186*, Harvard Business School, Boston, MA, rev. 21 July.

11 Sellers, P., *ibid.*

12 Reis, A., and Trout, J. (1994) "Don't follow the leader." *Marketing Management*, 25–26, February.

13 Reis, A. (1985) "Colas' thirst for battle." *Marketing*, 36–37, 21 November.

14 Sparks, D., *ibid.*, p. 27.

15 Sellers, P. (1978), *ibid.*

16 Sellers, P. (1994), *ibid.*

17 Dunkin, A. (1986) "Pepsi's marketing magic: Why nobody does it better." *Business Week*, 52–57, 10 February.

18 Sellers, P., *ibid.*

19 Reaves, L. (1986) "China market hot despite setbacks." *Advertising Age*, 56–60, 9 June.

20 Flagg, Michael (1999) "Pepsi siphons off some of Coke's lead in China by learning to pick its battles." *Wall Street Journal*, New York, 29 November.

21 Seligman, S. D. (1986) "Translating your trademark into Chinese." *The China Business Review*, 14–16, November-December.

22 Badenhausen, K. (1996) "There's nothing wrong with being no. 2." *Financial World*, p.29, 8 April.

23 Sellers, P. (1978), *ibid.*

24 McLean, B., *ibid.*

25 Bainbridge, J. (2000) "Global forces." *Marketing*, London, 20 July.

26 Scandic Hotels Year-End Reports, www.scandic-hotels.com.

27 Author interview, August 24, 2001.

Glossary

This chapter provides additional information on key thinkers in the area of decision making, and tools and resources. It includes a table of techniques for individual and group decision making, as well as one on tools for strategic analysis and decision making.

A FEW KEY THINKERS

Daniel Bernoulli (1700–1782) – The great Swiss physicist first introduced the concept of decision theory in 1738 (biography at (www-groups.dcs.st-andrews.ac.uk/~history/Mathematicians/Bernoulli_Daniel.html).

James G. March – Holds professorships in education, international management (Emeritus), political science, and sociology (Emeritus), at Stanford. His recent research focuses on understanding risk-taking, decision making, learning, and leadership in organizations such as universities. He is the creator of the "garbage can" model of decision making. His extensive publications include the 1994 book, *A Primer on Decision-Making*.

Henry Mintzberg – The John Cleghorn Professor of Management Studies at McGill University in Montreal. He is one of the great thinkers and writers on organizations, particularly in the area of strategy. His extensive publications include *The Rise and Fall of Strategic Planning*, which won the Academy of Management's best book award in 1995. His original work identified 10 managerial roles divided into three areas interpersonal, information, and decision making. His most recent thinking on managerial decision making adds "seeing first" and "doing first" as complements to the traditional "thinking first" approach.

Herbert A. Simon (1916–2001) – In 1978, he received the Alfred Nobel Memorial Prize in Economic Sciences for his work on decision making in economic organizations. Simon created a normative model of decision making which incorporated the groundbreaking idea that rationality is constrained, which he called "bounded rationality" (autobiography at www.nobel.se/economics/laureates/1978/simon-autobio.html).

Victor H. Vroom – Is the John G. Searle Professor of Organization and Management, Professor of Psychology, at Yale. He is famous for his contingency theory of decision making, and for the expectancy theory of motivation, as well as his extensive work on leadership. His books include the landmark *Work and Motivation*, and the groundbreaking *Leadership and Decision Making* and *The New Leadership*.

TOOLS, AND RESOURCES

Rational decision-making terms

Tom Spradlin (http://faculty.fuqua.duke.edu/daweb/lexicon.htm) clarifies common terms in the lexicon of rational decision making. For example, he distinguishes *decisions* (allocation of resources) from *objectives* (what the decision-maker hopes to achieve through the allocation of resources), and decision making from *prioritization* (which might be used as an aid in making certain decisions, or as a step that precedes making a decision). He also provides a useful discussion of other terms used in rational approaches, including terms associated with uncertainties (forecasts, probability distribution, expected value, and sensitivity), outcomes and value (direct vs indirect value, economic value, net present value, discount rate, and trade-offs), and risk (risk averse/risk neutral, certain equivalent vs expected NPV, and utility function).

Tools and techniques for individual and group decision making

As is the case with so many other areas of management, a whole host of tools and techniques have been invented over the years to help managers make better decisions. Some of these tools are very simple, some are more complex. Some are useful, others less so. How helpful any tool is, of course, depends on who is using it and for what purpose.

Brainstorming   (http://www.jpb.com/creative/brainstorming. html) – A well-known technique to help groups develop new ideas and approaches to problems. Group members are convened and encouraged to contribute any and all ideas that they may have, to combine and build upon the good ideas offered by others, and not to analyze, criticize, or otherwise interfere with the spontaneous flow of ideas. Volume, speed, and uninhibited flow of idea generation are paramount to the success of this technique.

Brown papering (process mapping) – A technique that can be useful in tracing what really happens in a process. Process mapping has a long history of service in clarifying and evaluating manufacturing processes. It aids the organization in discovering value-adding and waste-generating activities, and process bottlenecks.

Typically, process mapping involves interviewing the people who carry out the work at each stage to understand the main activities, information flows, and connections. The next stage is to pin up a long sheet of brown paper – usually between four and six meters long – and map out the process using post-it notes, sheets of paper, and key documents. The people originally interviewed are then invited to review their part of the process to ensure that what has been constructed is an accurate description.

Once this stage has been completed, the people involved in the process or affected by it are invited to "walk through the brown paper model," adding suggestions for improvements on post-it notes as they go. Once this has been done, the comments form the basis of the next stage: re-drawing the brown paper process diagram to eliminate problems. The beauty of this technique is that improvements can be tested by asking people to walk the new process, before any expensive final decisions are made.

In the past, the process was then transferred from the post-its and brown paper to various software programs, such as Visio and other 2-D CAD systems, MS PowerPoint, Excel, and Project. Transferring the information to any of these software programs was a painstaking task that often took several days. Today, a variety of sophisticated software tools are available to facilitate process-mapping in real-time (see the Resources section for details).

Decision tree (http://www.mindtools.com/dectree.html) – Probably the best known of all decision-making tools, a decision tree is a graphic representation of the options flowing from an initial decision or set of decisions. It is used to map out alternative courses of action and assess the implications (e.g. financial) of such decisions. Probabilities (otherwise known as educated guesses) are assigned to the likelihood of the consequences that each decision is expected to generate.

Delphi technique – This collective planning process is commonly used in marketing research and social surveys. It engages a number of physically dispersed experts (or managers) in contributing anonymous ideas or evaluations regarding a particular topic or issue via a series of rounds leading toward consensus. Each manager receives the results from the first round of responses. They then have a specified period of time to review and comment, prioritize issues, etc., and return their input for the second round. The process is repeated until consensus is reached. This technique may be helpful in situations where face-to-face conflict poses a significant obstacle, certain factions tend to dominate live discussions, and/or groupthink is in evidence (for additional information, see www.cce.cornell.edu/admin/program/documents/delphi. cfm).

Fishbone diagram (the Ishikawa method) – Named for its appearance, the fishbone diagram (originally invented by Professor Kaoru Ishikawa of the University of Tokyo, hence references to the "Ishikawa method") is a diagnostic tool. It helps the user to understand the relationship between cause and effect and is especially useful in situations where the causes of a problem or crisis cannot be easily measured. In such situations, a fishbone diagram can help clarify the major issues involved in a decision. To create a fishbone diagram:

» state the problem in a box on the right hand side of a blank sheet of paper (the fish's head);

» draw a horizontal line across the page coming out of the left of the box (the fish's spine);

» write each possible cause of the problem on a line at 45 degrees to the horizontal line (to make the fish's ribs);

» ask what might lie behind each of the possible reasons making up the ribs and add each new reason as smaller bones coming off the ribs; and

» assess the linkages between the main reasons and sub-reasons to understand how they might be connected or whether they are duplicated elsewhere on the diagram.

Flipping a coin – One of the oldest and perhaps most under-rated decision-making techniques, there's more to this technique than meets the eye. It's important to recognize that a tool is only as good as the purpose for which it is used. Flipping a coin is only effective as a tool when a decision involves choosing between competing alternatives. It has absolutely no diagnostic or analytical properties whatsoever, at least none that most management consultants would admit to.

In fact, in the hands of an accomplished decision-maker, a coin can be a much more subtle instrument than any of the other tools discussed in this chapter. Given that there is a 50:50 chance of getting heads or tails, only a fool, a gambler (or a desperate manager) would put their faith in the outcome of flipping a coin. But faced with a situation where you are unable to decide between two options, even after conducting an extensive analysis, it is surprising how effective the technique can be. Flipping a coin can tell you what your conscious mind cannot. It can tell you what your intuition is trying to say, and make your own gut reaction quite clear to you.

Flow chart – A pictorial representation of the flow of information, ideas, or components through a system. In business, a flow chart will typically be used to illustrate a process whether it is the physical process in a production line or the management process by which tasks are completed. Flow charts are an excellent way to make visible what is happening within a closed, intangible system. They can be used to:

» identify steps in a process that can be eliminated to reduce costs or save time;

» determine more efficient ways to order or organize the process; and

» see if the whole process needs to be re-engineered to bring it up to date, or even completely eliminated.

Mind map – A completely unstructured way to visually represent the various strands of a complex issue in order to generate ideas, and/or to communicate those ideas to others. First, the central idea, problem, or issue is written in the middle of a large sheet of paper. Next, ideas triggered by the main theme are represented as a series of lines coming out from the center, with subsidiary ideas or issues coming off these. It begins to look like a spider's web, or the root system of a tree, with lines spreading out towards the edge of the paper in all directions.

Mind mapping frees people from the need to order their thoughts or to impose prior logic. This allows them to approach problems quite literally with a blank sheet of paper. In many ways, mind mapping is the pictorial equivalent of brainstorming. (Go to www.tld.jcu.edu.au/netshare/learn/mindmap/index.html for a terrific guide to mind mapping.)

Nominal group technique – A technique for generating ideas, evaluating alternatives, and anonymously voting on solutions. Group members are convened to discuss a problem or issue. Once it has been discussed, each individual writes down his or her ideas for potential solutions, then offers one idea from their list to the group. Ideas are recorded on a flip chart without discussion in a series of rounds until all ideas have been shared. Then the group discusses the ideas and offers their agreement or disagreement. Each member may defend or criticize any idea. Group members then vote anonymously on their top three choices. The technique promotes balanced participation and representation (http://instruction.bus.wisc.edu/obdemo/readings/ngt.html, http://mason.gmu.edu/~falemi/cqi/nomial.htm).

Prioritization – There are many tools and techniques for helping managers prioritize. The ABC method is a common, simple, and effective approach. Pending tasks and decisions are designated as A, B, or C according to their level of importance and/or urgency, with A being top priority and/or most urgent. Thus a very important decision that need not be made until next week might be denoted as AB (A for very important and B for moderately urgent). In this way, managers can quickly determine the order in which they should tackle tasks. It also enables them to identify important decisions that might otherwise get put off because of more urgent but unimportant tasks.

Tools for strategic analysis and decision making

ABC analysis (Activity-Based Costing) – A relatively recent and important method of ensuring that all costs, and especially indirect costs and overheads, are properly allocated to particular products. Traditional costing methods allocated indirect costs via cost centers, which tended to under-allocate cost to special products and services that used a lot of indirect cost; it resulted in standard products being priced too high and specials too low. ABC better allocates indirect costs by identifying the cost drivers for each activity.

ABC can also be turned into an accounting system, but it is really a way of analyzing product profitability at a point in time. Since the cost drivers and activities can change, ABC analysis needs to be revisited periodically to ensure that the previous data and insights are still valid. ABC should lead to changed decisions about pricing, product and customer focus, market share policy, and other actions that can raise profitability.

OffTech Computing Pty Ltd., based in South Australia, offers the Activity Based Costing Portal, with helpful links, information, a magazine, and forums, all devoted to ABC (www.offtech.com.au/abc/Activity_Based_Costing.html).

ABM (Activity-Based Management) – An extension of ABC Analysis that takes customers' needs into consideration and determines where the extra cost of special products or services can be fully or more than fully recovered from customers. ABM has not yet achieved anything like the popularity of ABC, but it is a logical outgrowth of it and the focus on customer utility can be useful (see www.saffm.hq.af.mil/FMC/ABC/Definition.htm for a more detailed definition and overview, and www.icms.net for links to articles, books, and other resources on ABM).

Boston Matrix – A simple two-by-two matrix used for analyzing the strategic position of a particular business within a portfolio. It measures market growth and relative market share for all of the businesses in the company's portfolio. Each business can be placed on the matrix and classified as Stars (businesses with high growth rates and high market share), Cash Cows (low growth, high market share cash generators), Question Marks (high growth and low market share), or Dogs (the worst combination low market share and low growth). Decisions are then made as follows:

» Stars build
» Cash cows harvest
» Question Marks hold and monitor
» Dogs withdraw.

Cost-Benefit Analysis (CBA) – A monetary assessment of a project's worth that compares all of its costs and benefits. CBA is often used to assess public sector projects where an attempt is made to quantify social benefits. It can also be used by private sector managers to take account of *soft* benefits of a major project. Although less popular with the private sector, CBA can be used to evaluate projects that are thought to have major but indirect value, such as a corporate identity program. Even approximate quantification of soft benefits can be useful, provided CBA is not used to justify decisions already taken.

Porter's Five Competitive Forces – These five forces (the barriers to market entry, the threat of substitutes, the bargaining power of buyers and suppliers, and rivalry among existing competitors) provide a way for companies to understand the competitive markets in which they operate. They can be interpreted as the "rules of the game" that have to be acted on and challenged if a company is to change its competitive position within its marketplace. In other words, they are the levers upon which any strategy must act in order to be successful.

Scenario planning – Scenario planning may prove to be one of the most important decision-making tools in the manager's toolbox. It can be viewed as a way to facilitate lateral thinking in an organization. Although sometimes confused with disaster planning or contingency planning, which deals with how a company should respond when things go wrong, scenario planning is a way to identify both threats and opportunities that flow from decisions.

In effect, each scenario – or story about the future – may be conceived of as a different set of conditions in a "wind tunnel," and the policy or strategy decision as a prototype "aircraft" which must be tested in the wind tunnel to see how it performs under varying conditions. A decision may stand up well in one scenario, the argument goes, but the wings could drop off in another.

In writing scenarios, each should be a different story of the future with a different plot. There must be at least two scenarios and not more than four or five. Each scenario should be a detailed "story" of a possible future. The aim is not to predict the future, but to provide alternatives that can be used to "wind tunnel" strategies or plans.

SWOT analysis - Perhaps the best known and most basic of the analytic tools, SWOT analysis involves a review of Strengths, Weaknesses, Opportunities, and Threats. Generally, Strengths and Weaknesses will pertain to the organization itself; whereas Opportunities and Threats are more likely to arise from features of the external environment. SWOT analysis might be used, for example, when deciding whether to enter a new market in Eastern Europe. Through SWOT analysis, a clearer picture of the likely outcome of the decision should emerge.

The following tables categorize a variety of techniques and tools for individual and group decision making (Table 8.1) and for strategic analysis and decision making (Table 8.2).

Table 8.1 Techniques for individual and group decision-making.

| Technique | Levels of application | | | Ideas – action plans – solutions | | | | Temporal dimension | | Best For |
	Individual	Group	Organization	Generate	Evaluate	Prioritize		Synchronous	Asynchronous	
Brainstorming		X		X				X		Collectively generating large volume of ideas.
Brown papering (process mapping)		X	X		X			X	X	Process improvement involving all stakeholders.
Decision tree	X	X			X	X		X	X	Graphic representation and weighting of decision options.
Delphi technique		X	X	X	X	X			X	Obtaining consensus among dispersed experts where conflict and/or groupthink may be present.

Table 8.1 (Continued).

Technique	Levels of application			Ideas - action plans - solutions			Temporal dimension		Best For
	Individual	Group	Organization	Generate	Evaluate	Prioritize	Synchronous	Asynchronous	
Fishbone diagram	X	X			X		X		Clarifying inter-relationships among major issues in complex decisions.
Flipping a coin	X	X			X	X	X		Providing insight into one's own intuition when unable to decide.
Flow chart	X	X	X		X		X	X	Process improvement and re-engineering.
Mind map	X	X		X			X		Visual generation of ideas around a complex issue.
Nominal group technique		X		X	X	X	X		Balanced partici-pation and representation of all group members in decision process.
Prioritization	X					X	X		Determining the order in which tasks should be executed.

Table 8.2 Tools for strategic analysis and decision-making.

Technique	Levels of application			Ideas – action plans – solutions				Temporal dimension		Best For
	Individual	Group	Organization	Generate	Evaluate	Prioritize	Synchronous	Asynchronous		
ABC analysis (Activity-Based Costing)			X		X			X		Identifying cost drivers for each activity to better allocate costs.
ABM (Activity-Based Management)			X		X			X		Identifying and recovering from customers extra costs associated with special products and services.
Boston Matrix			X		X	X	X	X		Clarifying the strategic position of a business within a portfolio, and aligning actions to support it.

Table 8.2 Tools for strategic analysis and decision-making.

| Technique | Levels of application | | | Ideas – action plans – solutions | | | | Temporal dimension | | Best For |
	Individual	Group	Organization	Generate	Evaluate	Prioritize		Synchronous	Asynchronous	
Porter's Five Competitive Forces			X		X	X		X		Helping a company understand its competitive markets.
Scenario planning		X	X		X	X		X		"Test driving" one or more hypothetical decision scenarios.
SWOT analysis			X		X			X		Evaluating strengths, weaknesses, opportunities, and threats regarding a particular strategic decision.

Resources

Today the Web provides ready access to an increasing variety of high quality information, tools, and resources related to managerial decision making. This chapter provides descriptions of and links to Web-based knowledge portals; articles, books, and training resources; associations and organizations, and decision making and strategic analysis tools and support systems.

WEB-BASED KNOWLEDGE PORTALS

There are several gateways on the Web to extensive resources on various forms of decision support systems.

Appreciative Inquiry Resource E-Centre – created by Anne Radford in the UK, the editor of the global Ai Newsletter. This helpful site offers background information on Ai, international Ai resources, conferences, the quarterly newsletter (for a small fee), and a shopping mall for materials on Ai (www.aradford.co.uk/index.htm). The **Thin Book Publishing Company** in the US also sells books and articles on Ai and related topics. There is also a featured column with a recent article by an Ai practitioner (www.thinbook.com).

DSSResources.com – Dr Daniel J. Power, Professor of Information Systems and Management at the College of Business Administration at the University of Northern Iowa, Cedar Falls, Iowa, edits and manages this outstanding knowledge portal. The site provides extensive online articles, case studies, tutorials, decision aids, a glossary of terms used in the field, and links to vendors of DSS systems and other resources. It also provides information and links to closely related fields including artificial intelligence, business process reengineering, database and data warehousing, geographic information systems, groupware, human-computer interaction, management science, Bayesian decision tools, and software engineering. If you visit only one Website related to DSS, this must be it. Dan provides a "web-tour" for newcomers. It provides a helpful introduction to DSS and overview of the field. Viewing the information is free, but downloading or printing articles and case studies requires a nominal subscription ($10 for one month, $20 for three months, or $30 for six months) (http://dssresources.com).

Data Warehousing Information Center – This targeted knowledge portal is maintained by Larry Greenfield as an offshoot of his Chicago-based consultancy, LGI Systems Incorporated. The purpose of the site is to provide information and education for the layperson on data warehousing and decision support. It's primarily an informational site, and does not market any particular product or service. Larry strives to give a balanced view of data warehousing and decision support and to provide information to enable the reader to make up his or her own mind regarding data warehousing and decision support. For example, he provides cases both for and against data warehousing. The site offers a series of essays, links to vendors helpfully grouped into several categories, and links to additional resources and organizations (www.dwinfocenter.org).

The Natural Step – Excellent knowledge portals available in English for the US and Australia. The portals provide links to information on the NS framework, research about TNS, case summaries, a newsletter, educational videos, and information on upcoming summits and events. In the US, TNS "conducts multidisciplinary research, provides tailored consulting and training services, and offers networking and educational opportunities for leaders, organizations, and communities interested in creating sustainability agendas and initiatives" (www.naturalstep.org). Australia's Website provides a similar bounty of online resources (members.ozemail. com.au/~natstep/).

ARTICLES, BOOKS, AND TRAINING RESOURCES

Decision analysis – For a short list of recent books, articles and chapters on this topic, with a focus on decision analysis in the healthcare and legal industries, go to www.treeage.com/products/rsrc.htm.

For an extensive list of links to both academic and commercial Websites pertaining to decision analysis, go to www.sjdm.org/related-links.shtml.

Decision-making and problem-solving – HRDQ, a managerial training and development organization based in King of Prussia, Pennsylvania, provides an extensive online store with product offerings helpfully categorized (http://www.hrdq.com/default.htm). Selecting "decision-making" from the drop-down menu under workshops and programs yields resources for managers and consultants ranging from force field analysis to profiles on intuitive decision making, participative management, consensus building, and problem-solving styles. HRDQ online is easily searchable and covers an extensive list of management topics in addition to decision making. It is, however, but one of many companies with such Web-based offerings on the Web.

Organization charts – For links to Internet resources and books relating to the design and use of business and non-business related

charts, go to www.smartdraw.com/drawing/orgcharts/resources.
htm. The page is designed to provide information to support
use of the award-winning SmartDraw graphic software (see
"Fishbone/Ishikawa diagrams" below for additional information).

Associations and organizations

Activity Based Costing Benchmarking Association – A free
association of individuals who work with Activity Based Costing and
Benchmarking, and organizations that subscribe to the Association's
mission, goals, and operating guidelines. The Website provides
an extensive set of links to benchmarking associations that
are arranged according to their focus on specific industries
or processes. The organization also provides virtual and live
roundtable discussions throughout the year on various aspects
of ABC processes, as well as a variety of benchmarking studies
(www.abcbenchmarking.com).

DAS (Decision Analysis Society) – DAS is one of the largest subdi-
visions of INFORMS (Institute for Operations Research and the
Management Sciences), the world's largest organization of operations researchers and management scientists. DAS was originally
founded in 1980 as a special interest group within the Operations
Research Society of America. The site also offers course syllabi
on decision analysis, links to relevant journals, and to abstracts of
working papers in the field (faculty.fuqua.duke.edu/daweb).

Data Warehousing Institute – is the Website for the premier professional association for data warehousing and business intelligence
professionals. It provides a host of useful resources for the professional as well as the layperson. There are links to excellent case
studies on successful data warehousing implementations arranged
by industry, ranging from manufacturing, technology, and utilities, to
healthcare, legal, and financial. While some are fairly technical, most
are comprehensible to the non-professional, and can provide helpful
overviews of a variety of industry-specific applications (www.dw-
institute.com).

International Society for Decision Support Systems – If you're
not yet feeling totally overwhelmed with the plethora of resources,
associations, concepts, applications, and questions swirling around

decision science and DSS, try visiting this international (based in Texas) society's Website for pages of links (possibly in the hundreds) to journals and online publications from around the world that pertain to various aspects of the field. You'll need to develop a decision support system just to help you determine which journal(s) to investigate (http://www.uky.edu/BusinessEconomics/dssakba/periodcl. htm).

The site also offers an equally overwhelming array of links to vendors of DSS software, and to instructional software, applications, and cases arranged by application categories, including DSS for decisions on careers, education, finance, group support, health, information technology, insurance, investments, the law, life, natural resources, purchasing, real estate, relocation, retirement, taxes, travel, etc., etc. Do not doubt that DSS is having an impact on various aspects of your life, whether you know it or not.

SJDM (Society for Judgment and Decision-Making) – SJDM started out as an informal association in 1981 and was formally instituted in 1986 as an interdisciplinary academic society focused on the study of normative, descriptive, and prescriptive decision theories. Resources available to non-members online include links to an extensive series of courses on decision making. Course offerings range from "Human Judgment and Decision-Making," "Group Processes in Decision Making, Problem Solving, and Judgment," and "Managerial Decision-Making," to "Decision-Making in Government and Administration." The site also offers a list of dissertations published in the field since 1994, a searchable database of references to books and chapters on judgment and decision making, and links to journals, academic programs, and other organizations related to the field (http://www.sjdm.org/index. shtml).

EADM (European Association for Decision-Making) – "An interdisciplinary organization dedicated to the study of normative, descriptive, and prescriptive theories of decision." The association is based in Leiden, the Netherlands, and dates back to 1969. The association sponsors biannual conferences, produces a bulletin three times a year, and offers an electronic mailing list, among other services (www.psy.uva.nl/ResEdu/EADM/home.html).

DECISION-MAKING AND STRATEGIC ANALYSIS TOOLS AND SUPPORT SYSTEMS

ABC (Activity-Based Costing) – Acorn Systems Inc. offers one example of software designed to support ABC analysis (www.acornsys. com/Solutions/Solutions_Qabc.htm). The software enables a company to quickly assess the profitability of customers, products, suppliers, and even specific orders and line items. Detailed reports may be generated on operations, sales, and/or marketing. Possibilities include product, route, and vendor profitability, scorecards on facilities, product categories, sales reps, territories, and customer types, and customer and pricing matrices, among others.

In addition to the rapid growth of powerful software programs that facilitate the implementation of ABC, perhaps the most significant, cutting-edge change is one that such software has enabled. ABC analysis is being transformed from a somewhat dull annual manufacturing-oriented chore into a vital real-time decision-making support that gives managers an ongoing, process-oriented picture of their product, channel, and customer profitability. Armstrong Laing Group, one of the world's leading providers of ABC software, is on the cutting edge of this change. It has combined its "advanced activity-based costing engine, Metify ABM, with Web-based data collection, online analytical processing, and graphical reporting tools to create an executive performance dashboard" (www.metify.com).

ABM (Activity Based Management) – ICMS (Integrated Cost Management Systems) based in Arlington, Texas, provides ABM software, live and Web-based ABM training, extensive links to articles, books and other resources on ABM, 10 principles of ABM, and more. They service top tier clients in industry, government, services, and associations (www.icms.net).

Boston Matrix – The Marketing Process Company provides an online tutorial to working with the Boston Matrix (www.themarketing processco.com/e-brochures/boston_matrix_tutorial/mpc_bm_e-broch. htm). The company, based in Burnam, Buckinghamshire, UK, evolved out of a 1994 collaboration with Professor Malcolm McDonald and Cranfield University's School of Management to develop their EXMAR strategic marketing planning software. They work with clients in over 30 countries and a wide range of industries.

Brainstorming – Visual brainstorming tools are closely related to mind mapping software (see below). In contrast, DSS Infotech Pvt. Ltd., an ISO 9001 certified software consultancy out of Pune, India, offers a linearly-structured, primarily text-based collective brainstorming tool called Solutions Genie (www.brainstormingdss.com/index.html). Each participant enters ideas into their networked computer on the topic being brainstormed. The software provides support not only for idea generation, but also for selection among generated ideas through a variety of decision-making applications.

Brown papering/Process mapping – A wide variety of software tools and specialized products and services are now available to support process mapping in various industries. "ActiveModeler," offered by TQS Europe, is one sophisticated example (www.tqseu rope.com/activemo.htm). The program models the way people actually work together in organizations. It enables you to capture factors ranging from labor cost and wait times, to relationships between processes, work roles, and departments. Resulting process maps can be published on the Internet or corporate intranet, thus transforming them into valuable corporate assets.

ActiveModeler also makes it possible to analyze and contrast different scenarios, perform role cost modeling, and conduct simulations via a real-time event generator. Last but certainly not least, workflow extensions permit the software to actually control and execute workflow in the designated processes. This is but one example of the wide range of process-mapping software tools now available. Decision-making tools have come a *long* way. Brown paper and post-it notes, anyone?

Decision trees – Similarly, decision tree tools have crawled out of the paper-and-pencil primordial soup and continue to evolve into high-powered decision-support software. For example, Vanguard Software Corporation builds the latest decision-science technologies into its software, DecisionScript and DecisionPro (www.vanguardsw.com). DecisionPro enables the user to quickly and easily generate decision trees without having to enter any formulas. In addition to decision-tree analysis, it integrates other managerial decision-making capabilities including Monte Carlo simulations, linear programming, and advanced forecasting methods. It's been referred to as "the Swiss army knife of decision analysis."

DATA (Decision Analysis by TreeAge Software Inc.) is a very popular DSS used in a wide range of industries ranging from chemicals, pharmaceuticals, and energy production to banking, legal, and healthcare. It's also popular among leading business schools in Europe, Japan, Canada, and the US. Versions of DATA are available for both PCs and Macs. DATA incorporates a variety of complex tools for analysis and model building as aids to decision making (www.treeage.com).

Decision trees are also being employed in increasingly complicated ways in data mining programs, artificial intelligence, and other computer learning applications.

Fishbone/Ishikawa diagrams, flow charts, and other business diagrams – SmartDraw is a multiple award-winning graphics program that makes it easy to create a bewildering array of business and non-business related diagrams (www.smartdraw.com). Possibilities range from flow charts and fishbone diagrams to Gantt and organizational charts, timelines, technical drawings, and software maps, among hundreds of others.

Mind mapping – Now you can create mind maps on your personal computer with a variety of useful applications ranging from brainstorming to decision making (www.mindmapper.com/your.htm).

Mind Manager is an elegant, award-winning "visual thinking tool" software that helps you generate, organize, and colorfully display your web of ideas on a particular topic. Business and educational applications are now available through MindJet (www.mindjet.com). The site may be viewed in English or German.

Prioritization – Computerized prioritization tools are rapidly becoming de rigeur in areas of extreme complexity, for example assessing levels of environmental risk for multiple sites, projects, and processes in heavy industry and utilities. One of many such resources available online is through Strategic Corporate Assessment Systems, a privately held company with bases in Australia and North America (www.strategicorp.com). The site may be viewed in English, French, German, Italian, Japanese, Portuguese, and Spanish.

Ten Steps to Effective Decision Making

The meaning of effectiveness in managerial decision making is explored. Next, the characteristics of effective decisions are identified, and the barriers to abandoning faulty decisions are discussed. Research findings that provide clues to improving the effectiveness of managerial decision making are then presented, followed by ten guidelines to support effective decision making.

- » What makes a decision "effective?"
- » Barriers to abandoning a faulty decision
- » Enhancing the effectiveness of managerial decision making
- » Ten steps to effective decision making

"Every decision is wrong given enough time. I believe that to be true, because there is no decision that is right for all time."

J.D. Eveland

In this chapter we'll begin by considering the meaning of effectiveness in managerial decision making. We'll identify the characteristics of effective managerial decisions and the barriers to abandoning faulty decisions. We'll then consider research findings that provide clues to improving the effectiveness of managerial decision making, and conclude by sharing ten guidelines that support effective decision making.

WHAT MAKES A DECISION "EFFECTIVE?"

What exactly is an "effective" decision? As the Coke vs Pepsi case in Chapter 7 illustrates, it all depends. First, it depends on your perspective. Are you looking for a win-win or win-lose solution? Are you focused solely on self-interest, or on how your decisions impact larger systems as well, like the environment? And what works well for another manager or organization simply may not work for you or yours. It may not fit your personality, values, or style. It may not fit your organization's values or culture, even though it may otherwise be a valid approach.

Second, it depends on your particular criteria for success. Do you need to optimize the outcome in this situation, or will satisficing do? Are you monitoring only bottom line results, or looking for holistic confirmation (see Chapter 6, "A spiritual compass for decision making")? Do your criteria address the needs of all stakeholders, or only a select few?

Third, it depends on the relevant timeframe. For example, J.D. Eveland offers another thought-provoking aphorism:[1] "the longer a given decision is successful, the greater the chances that it will fail catastrophically." He explains "I think that's probably true too. The sooner you realize the boundaries of the effectiveness of your decision, the easier it is to make changes to it. The longer it has good consequences, the more wedded to it you become, and the harder it becomes to change it." It can be hard to change course even when a decision has bad consequences (see "Barriers to abandoning a faulty decision" below).

Eveland continues "I'm not sure if there's any such thing as a good decision, because every decision is time bound. What seems to be a really good decision at the time, there's no guarantee that five years later you'll still think it was a good decision. There's no guarantee that the decisions we're making now are all that much better – they're just the best decisions we can make right now under the circumstances." Does the fact that a decision may be the best one that we are capable of making right now make it an "effective" decision? Perhaps. It all depends on your perspective(s), criteria, timeframe, and. . .

Fourth, it depends upon the degree to which the decision is successfully implemented. Clearly a non-implemented decision is not particularly effective. But how effective is a partially or poorly or haphazardly implemented decision? As discussed in Chapter 1, in his 1999 study of 356 highly diverse, actual executive decisions, Paul Nutt defined the "success" of a decision as the degree to which the decision is fully implemented over an extended period of time (which he specified as a two year period in that study).[2]

Fifth, this assumes that, at the very least, a decision gets made – even if it's a conscious choice *not* to act for a few hours or a few days or weeks, or to *not* proceed with a pre-set plan of action. A conscious decision not to act is a powerful and decisive act in and of itself – especially when buffeted by intense pressures from others who are addicted to the illusion of the superiority of speedy action. It requires being anchored in a state of inner calm – the eye in the midst of the storm – that may be nurtured through contemplative practice.

A conscious decision not to act differs markedly from *indecision*, the scourge of managerial decision-makers. Indecision is essentially the avoidance of commitment to a specific course of action – or non-action – out of fear, insecurity, doubt, and so on. Indecision may also result from a mental "logjam" in which a manager's brain becomes overwhelmed with the wildly entangled branches resulting from multiple decision trees and analyses. Visible indicators include steam rising from the top of the beleaguered manager's head. This is an excellent time to "turn within," and to engage in centering prayer, meditation, and/or exercise.

But let's assume that a decision does get made *and* "successfully" implemented – that is, fully implemented for an extended period of time. What if turns out to be the *"wrong"* decision? The American general George Patton reputedly had something to say about this: "the best decision is the right one, second best is the wrong one, and worst is no decision." How could a wrong decision be better than no decision? Patton may have been thinking about maintaining the appearance of the self-assured leader, which certainly has is merits. However, fully committing to a decision that turns out wrong may also hasten the speed with which you realize that it's a wrong decision, and theoretically enables you to abandon that erroneous course of action and move on to a more advantageous one. It permits learning from one's mistakes. Indecision indefinitely postpones the pain that may be associated with such constructive learning.

In order for learning from "wrong" decisions to occur, however, it is essential that the organizational culture support risk-taking. This involves creating an environment in which learning from mistakes is valued as much as learning from success, in which safety mechanisms are established to protect those who have the courage to take risks (within certain mutually agreed upon limits), and incentives are established to encourage calculated risk-taking and learning from those experiences.

BARRIERS TO ABANDONING A FAULTY DECISION

The notion that a decision-maker will abandon or change their course of action once they discover that a decision is flawed or wrong, however, is complicated by at least two phenomena: escalation of commitment, and groupthink. Escalation of commitment refers to the tendency to continue an ineffective course of action once it becomes evident that the situation cannot be turned around. Most of us have experienced this in one form or another. We continue to spend time, money, or other resources on a project (or relationship) that shows less and less promise of delivering the results that we'd hoped for. Sometimes we've put our hearts and souls into it, and it's hard for us to accept the idea that it may never pay off.

Ross and Staw[3] identify four underlying factors involved in escalation of commitment:

1. psychological and social factors such as saving face, peer pressure, and ego defense;

2 project-related factors, for example attributing ongoing setbacks in a
   project to temporary causes, or delayed return on project investment;
3 organizational factors such as inertia and politics; and
4 environmental factors, for example political pressure.

They also offer suggestions on ways to reduce the potential for escalation of commitment. Interestingly, one of these suggestions is the same
as a key suggestion for creating a culture that promotes learning from
mistakes: reduce the risks and penalties associated with failures. By
doing so, the organization makes failure a viable option. It helps relieve
those responsible for a sinking project of having to resort to desperate
and costly heroics to try to rescue it from inevitable disaster.

Other suggestions focus on the importance of providing regular
feedback regarding project completion criteria, progress, and costs,
as well as the escalating costs associated with continuing the current
course of action. Another creative suggestion is to give the responsibility
for deciding the fate of the project to different managers at different
points in time.

In highly cohesive decision-making groups, groupthink[4] can come
into play. Irving Janis originally coined the term groupthink to describe
flawed decision-making processes he discovered while analyzing various US foreign policy debacles such as the Vietnam War. Groupthink
occurs when a decision-making group becomes so cohesive that it
suppresses dissenters and disconfirming evidence as it unanimously
supports a notably ill-conceived decision. What seems to happen is that
once beliefs achieve a certain critical mass in the group they become
"accepted truths" – whether validated or not – within the group. This
makes it difficult to challenge those "truths" even when the conditions
that gave rise to them change.

The dangers of groupthink have been well documented in numerous
famous cases as well as in laboratory studies. In particular, groupthink
can cause the following:

» inadequate exploration of the issues;
» tendency to accept received wisdom of the group without challenging its validity;
» over reliance on biased supporting evidence;
» discussion constrained by group norms;

» inability to think outside the box;
» social pressure not to rock the boat;
» failure to ask what could go wrong or to make contingency plans; and
» the decision-making process is often little more than a case of "going through the motions" to arrive at a predetermined outcome.

One way to offset the impact of groupthink is to deliberately include a dissenting voice in the decision making group. More enlightened leaders use this technique to encourage alternative options when faced with important decisions. For example, Lee Iacocca, when he was CEO of Chrysler, would often appoint a "contrarian" at important meetings to make sure he had a dissenting voice present to state the other side of the argument. But other organizations are less receptive to criticism. Warren Bennis, the American management guru, once said that seven out of ten executives in America's top companies do not speak up when they think the boss has got it wrong.

Fortunately, Janis[5] and others offer suggestions for preventing and counter-acting groupthink, including, among others:

» assign someone to play "devil's advocate" – to be a dissenting voice;
» encourage all group members to voice doubts and objections;
» use different groups with different leaders to consider the same decision;
» have everyone rethink their positions once a consensus has been reached; and
» use subgroup debates and outside experts to help generate alternative perspectives.

ENHANCING THE EFFECTIVENESS OF MANAGERIAL DECISION MAKING

Paul Nutt[6] found that some managerial approaches to decision making are significantly more effective than others, but that managers use them less frequently. His research focused on three key action stages in the decision-making process: establishing direction, identifying options, and implementation. In each stage he identified managerial tactics that were much more successful than others.

The two most successful approaches to establishing direction were found to be setting objectives and intervening in the process. Intervening was substantially more successful than setting objectives, problem-solving, or running with an idea (e.g. 92% vs 58%, 44%, and 42% full use rates, respectively), yet it was the least frequently used approach. Intervening involves benchmarking the performance levels of multiple respected organizations in the same field, establishing new norms for performance, extensive networking with key stakeholders, documenting performance against the new norms, and so on. Setting objectives – communicating desired goals that leave a lot of room for creative alternative solutions – is "commonly known, but uncommonly practiced because managers often have a bias toward action and fear being seen as indecisive."

When identifying options in the decision-making process, developing *multiple options* was found to substantially increase their decision-making effectiveness (from 56% to 70%), yet managers developed multiple options in fewer than 1 out of 5 decisions that they made. Finally, intervention and participation were highly effective approaches to implementation, in some cases nearly double the success rates for implementation via persuasion or edict (the least effective yet most widely used approaches). And the more comprehensive the participation of stakeholders, the more successful the implementation was found to be (as high as 100% sustained use rate over a two year period for cases involving complete participation of stakeholders).

TEN STEPS TO EFFECTIVE DECISION MAKING

We are finally ready to unveil the long-awaited ten steps. Of course, as the preceding chapters have illustrated, decision making is as much art and craft as science, and masterpieces of art or craft are not byproducts of paint-by-numbers. Do not consider these steps as a blueprint, but rather as a palette of guidelines to draw upon when creating your own masterworks of managerial decisions.

1 *Do what works*. Painfully obvious, yet so many managers fail to do just that. Edicts and persuasion don't work well; you now have evidence. Reduce your dependence on them. You're better off with a coin toss. Try things that have been shown to work, even if it may

be uncomfortable for you to do so at first: intervene, set objectives, be sure to identify *multiple* options, and involve all those who have a stake in the potential outcomes of the decision. Get coached by someone who has successfully used these approaches.

2 *Ask the right questions*. Right from the very beginning. What do you *really want?* The way you frame your initial questions will shape and influence all aspects of the decision process that follows. Play with them, mull them over – not just by yourself, but with as many other people who have a vested interest in the outcomes as possible. Think: do you only want to reduce or eliminate unwanted conditions, for example like sexual harassment complaints, or do you really want something far beyond that, like mutually respectful, high quality working relationships between men and women in the workplace?[7] The first question is likely to set you on a course of identifying and ferreting out undesirable behaviors, establishing policies to forbid them, and training all employees on what you *don't want* – which in this example is likely to leave a legacy of fear, inter-gender hostility, and repression in its wake. So at the very outset, make sure you are working toward a future that you and your organization truly desire, not merely one that you don't want.

3 *Enter and engage the decision process from a centered place*. This requires an ability to develop an inner tranquility that you bring with you into your daily life. It becomes an incredible contribution in the midst of the turbulence and turmoil that surround high-stakes managerial decision making. There are many ways to develop this sense of calm. Yoga, tai chi, some other forms of exercise, meditation, prayer, and quiet reflection on profoundly meaningful and/or sacred writing, among others. Develop a contemplative practice that works for you. It may even help lower your blood pressure, as well as of those who work with you.

4 *Listen*. To what you want to hear, and to what you don't. To those you want to hear, and to those you don't. Listen inwardly as well as outwardly. Get to know your own sense of intuition, and listen to it, especially in volatile situations.

5 *Involve others*. Right from the outset, and in full voice, not simply as token advisors, or to rubber stamp a decision you've already made. Be sure to include the voices that are not often heard – and

that have a stake in the result. Broaden the scope of participation as widely as possible in situations in which participation is called for. Keep in mind that participation is one of the primary approaches to effective implementation. After all, what good is a non-implemented decision? Try thinking through the questions in Vroom, Yetton, and Jago's Decision-Making Model (see Chapter 2) to help you determine the extent to which others need to be included in a particular decision process.

6 *Learn from the best*. The best examples, stories, products, services, people, practices, and organizations. Catch them doing something right, and acknowledge them for it. As you hone your ability to ask the right questions, you will be led on a search for the excellent, the extraordinary, the meaningful, and the wildly successful – on all levels, holistically. You'll discover those who are having their cake *and* eating it too. Apply this to learning from mistakes as well. What are the absolute *best lessons* that we can learn from our mistakes? What are the outstanding qualities that people brought to the project they were working on even though it may have failed – the qualities that you want to celebrate and make sure that you express throughout your organization now and in the future?

7 *Create easy access to high quality data*. It's a key contributor to effective decision making in today's complex infocracies. Keep in mind that once you start asking for what you really want as opposed to merely what you don't want, which leads you on a treasure hunt for the best, you may have to create new metrics to support you in tracking those events, practices, procedures, behaviors, and so on. Make sure the information that you are gathering is the right information – the information that will support you in getting to where you really want to go. Then share that data with all relevant stakeholders. Put it in the hands of those closest to ongoing decision opportunities. Make meaning from the data collaboratively in order to generate unique insights and points of view from the same data.

8 *Include the bigger picture; include the planet*. You and your organization are either contributing to a sustainable future for the planet, or not. Join the winning global team. Learn the basics about sustainability. Involve your entire organization and community. Develop a competitive advantage out of it, as Scandic Hotels, Ikea,

and many others are doing. Fully integrate it as a vital component of your strategic decision-making processes. As your organization becomes fully engaged and builds on its successes, push it through your supply chain. Have an impact that future generations, even your grandchildren, will be proud of – and live to see, thanks to the actions of you and millions of others like you. It is possible to design your business in the direction of sustainability. Just do it. Time is of the essence, and we don't have another planet to go to.

9 *Make implementation your mantra*. As you ask the right questions, involve others, learn from the best, include the bigger picture, get the data you need, and stay centered, think implementation. See it; feel it. Make it your mantra, right from the beginning. "Implement, implement, implement, implement... " Forget the idea that you make decisions and others implement. It doesn't work. Get involved in the entire process. Provide leadership, coaching, resources, and support. Bring enthusiasm, confidence in the abilities of others, and healthy questioning. You don't have to do it all, but you have to be an integral part of it.

10 *Be brave, be humble, and share the pain and the glory*. Have the courage to change, the courage to decide – even if the decision is not to act. Humility is based on a healthy sense of one's own limitations. This is especially critical when you are entrusted with the lives and well being of others. Awareness of one's limitations extends to the awareness of the limitations of one's data, expert opinions, decision-support systems, tools, and techniques. Know that no matter how well you may have done your homework, you cannot eliminate risk or control the future. You can, however, learn to dance with it.

Finally, be human with your fellows. Change can be painful. Don't bite the bullet in silence. As a leader, let people know that you are human too. Share your concerns, and make it safe for them to express theirs as well. You can avoid a *lot* of trouble down the line that way. Pay close attention to holistic confirmation. What's your gut feel? If it all feels great, share the credit. Express your appreciation in public and one-on-one. Celebrate your successes, together. None of us succeed alone.

Like Mike Aristedes (see Chapter 6), we're all in the coin-tossing business, and it takes a lot to get there. We *can* improve the effectiveness of our managerial decision making. If we have the courage, common sense, patience, and perseverance to incorporate these ten guidelines into our decision making over time, we will improve its effectiveness. Given the challenges of the twenty-first century, we must.

KEY LEARNING POINTS

Decision effectiveness is influenced by:

- » perspectives
- » success criteria
- » timeframes
- » a decision being made
- » degree of implementation.

Barriers to abandoning a faulty decision:

- » escalation of commitment
- » groupthink.

Ten steps to effective decision making:

1. Do what works.
2. Ask the right questions.
3. Center yourself.
4. Listen.
5. Involve others.
6. Learn from the best.
7. Create easy access to high quality data.
8. Include the bigger picture and the planet.
9. Make implementation your mantra.
10. Be brave, be humble, and share the pain and the glory.

NOTES

1 Author interview.
2 Nutt, Paul, (1999) "Surprising but true: Half the decisions in organizations fail." *Academy of Management Executive* **13**(4).

3 Ross, J, and Staw, B. M. (1993) "Organizational escalation and exit: Lessons from the Shoreham nuclear power plant." *Academy of Management Journal*, August 1993, pp. 701–32.

4 Janis, I. (1982) *Groupthink*, 2nd edn. Houghton Mifflin, Boston.

5 Janis, I. (1982), *ibid.*

6 Nutt, P. (1999), *ibid.*

7 This is adapted from a story about one of David Cooperrider's consulting projects.

Frequently Asked Questions (FAQs)

Q1: How is decision making defined?

A: See Chapter 2, the sections on "Defining decision making" and "Nature, scope, and types of managerial decisions."

Q2: Why do so many significant managerial decisions fail?

A: See the discussion on Paul Nutt's research findings in Chapter 1.

Q3: How can managers improve their chances for success when implementing decision support systems?

A: See Chapter 4, the section on "Reducing high failure rates in DSS implementations," and Chapter 7, the section entitled "Best Buy - award winning success with DSS."

Q4: What is an "infocracy," and how does it impact making business decisions?

A: See Chapter 3, the section on "From bureaucracies to 'infocracies'."

Q5: How do cultural differences influence decision-making processes in organizations?

A: See Chapter 5, the section on "Cultural diversity in decision making."

Q6: What role, if any, should intuition play in making business decisions?

A: See Chapter 6, the section on "Complementing rationality with intuition."

Q7: How do executives draw upon their spirituality when making business decisions?

A: See Chapter 6, the section on "A spiritual compass for decision making."

Q8: How can commitment to global environmental and social concerns contribute to business success?

A: See Chapter 6, the section entitled "A global compass for managerial decision making," and Chapter 7, the section entitled "Values-centered decision support: Scandic Hotels."

Q9: What makes a decision "effective," or not?

A: See Chapter 10, the section on "What makes a decision 'effective'?" and Chapter 7, the section entitled "Successful strategic decision making: Coke vs Pepsi in China."

Q10: Where can I find some of the best information and resources on business decision making online?

A: See Chapter 9, Resources.

Acknowledgments

Writing one's first book is a daunting and exciting challenge. THANK YOU to everyone who helped make it possible:

» Capstone Publishing and Suntop Media – for providing the opportunity.
» Stuart Crainer and Des Dearlove – for their faith in me, patience, and ongoing encouragement.
» Richard Walshe – for his care in copy editing.
» Tom Fryer of Sparks Computer Solutions Ltd – for neatly expediting the process from first draft to press.
» Tom Brown – for seeing the writer in me and encouraging me to unleash it.
» Ken Murrell – for being such a great, empowering mentor.
» Janis Fitzgerald – for her enthusiasm and emotional support.
» Richard Clark – for helping me discover insights into my own decision-making nemeses.
» All of the interviewees – for their responsiveness, flexibility, insight, and inspiration.
» All of the business thinkers and researchers who pondered the vagaries of managerial decision-making for decades.
» And especially to all those who grapple with tough business decisions every day of their working lives.

Index

Printed and bound in the UK by
CPI Antony Rowe, Eastbourne

Printed and bound by CPI Group (UK) Ltd, Croydon, CR0 4YY

13/04/2025

14656564-0003